The Baptism and Gifts
of the Holy Spirit

The Baptism and Gifts of the Holy Spirit

By

MERRILL F. UNGER

MOODY PRESS
CHICAGO

Library of Congress Catalog Card Number: 74-2931

ISBN: 0-8024-0467-7

Third Printing, 1976

Printed in the United States of America

Contents

CHAPTER		PAGE
1.	The Baptism of the Spirit in Charismatic Christianity	7
2.	The Baptism of the Spirit Misunderstood	21
3.	The Baptism of the Spirit in the Gospels	39
4.	The Baptism of the Spirit at Pentecost and at Samaria	59
5.	The Baptism of the Spirit at Caesarea and Ephesus	81
6.	The Baptism of the Spirit in 1 Corinthians, Romans, and Galatians	95
7.	The Baptism of the Spirit in Ephesians, Colossians, and 1 Peter	117
8.	The Baptism of the Spirit and the Gifts of the Spirit	133
9.	The Baptism of the Holy Spirit and Power	147
	Notes	173
	Bibliography	181

1

The Baptism of the Spirit in Charismatic Christianity

ONE OF THE MOST NOTEWORTHY features of twentieth-century Christianity is the rise of a strong charismatic movement within the church. Appearing in various forms, this species of revivalism has one common basic element. It highlights the baptism of the Spirit, which it construes as an experience of power subsequent to salvation and maintains the evidence of this experience is speaking in tongues.[1]

By *tongues,* glossolalists usually mean genuine languages never learned but supernaturally spoken. Some, however, hold to the tenuous theory of an unknown tongue. This is imagined to be a special ecstatic utterance of the Spirit, not translatable and not understandable by men.[2] In any case, aside from the nature of the phenomenon, such a manifestation is called a charisma (from the Greek *charisma,* a gift), denoting an extraordinary power possessed by some of the early Christians.

Hence the term *charismatic* refers to such charismata as miracles of healing and supernatural utterance in languages. Such charismata, of course, took place in the apostolic church. Present-day charismatic revivalism holds that the same manifestations of the Spirit that appeared in the first century ought to be manifested today.[3]

Moreover, charismatic Christians contend that such manifestations do take place today when believers "receive the baptism of the Spirit" and the power it professedly brings with it.[4]

THE RISE OF CHARISMATIC CHRISTIANITY

1. *Pentecostalism has its roots in early Methodism of the eighteenth century and the revivalism of Charles G. Finney in the first half of the nineteenth century.*

"Eighteenth-century Methodism," as Frederick Dale Bruner correctly points out, "is the mother of the nineteenth-century American holiness movement which, in turn, bore twentieth-century Pentecostalism."[5] John Wesley taught a definite second work of grace distinct from the remission of sins.[6] By laying special emphasis upon such an instantaneous experience of sanctification subsequent to regeneration, Wesley preveniently prepared the way for the Pentecostal concept of a crisis and conscious experience of "the baptism of the Holy Spirit" following conversion.

American revivalism of the nineteenth century, particularly as exemplified in the doctrine and methods of Charles G. Finney (1792-1876), exerted a wide influence in shaping American Christianity and in turn became the major historical bridge between early Methodism and modern Pentecostalism.

Finney's theology embraced an experience subsequent to conversion which he styled "the baptism of the Holy Spirit."[7] His one-volume systematic theology is widely used today in Pentecostal circles and considered standard by the average Pentecostal evangelist and pastor.

However, even more influential on American Christianity than Finney's theology were his revival methods. These were purposely emotional and geared to high excitement. Finney justified his approach to bringing people to a spiritual crisis by the belief that "men are so sluggish." "There are so many things to lead their minds off from religion and to oppose the influence of the gospel that it is necessary to raise an excitement among them till the tide rises so high as to sweep away the opposing obstacles."[8]

By the middle of the nineteenth century, Finney's theology—which was essentially Methodism—his highly emotional revivalism had been transformed from a minority to a majority faith, to become, as McGloughlin points out, "the national religion of the United States.'"⁹ This meant that Finney's teaching of a spiritual baptism subsequent to conversion and his encouragement of high emotionalism in revival methodology had become prominent features of American Christianity. Both of these elements were later to find a permanent place in the Pentecostal movement of the twentieth century.

2. *Pentecostalism developed out of the holiness movement of the latter half of the nineteenth century.*

This second-blessing holiness phenomenon was largely Methodist—led by Methodists and appealing mainly to Methodists.[10] It was the outgrowth of the dissatisfaction of many within Methodist churches with the worldliness of the church as a whole and the lack of adherence to the Wesleyan doctrine of perfection.

The holiness movement, in loyalty to its Wesleyan heritage, found its theological center in a second experience after conversion. This was often dubbed by different terms: a pure heart, sanctification, perfection, or perfect love. But by whatever terminology it was called, it assured the so-called subsequent experience an importance it was later to assume in Pentecostalism.

In the holiness movement the phrase *the baptism of the Holy Spirit*—which was destined to have such wide significance in Pentecostal teaching—as the Pentecostal historian Kendrick confesses, "was popularized as the name for the experience of sanctification or 'second blessing.' All who came under the Holiness ministry became familiar with 'spiritual baptism.' "[11]

One of the chief protagonists of the holiness movement, W. E. Boardman, succinctly epitomized broad holiness principles as they later came to undergird distinctive Pentecostal tenets, when he wrote, "There is a *second experience* distinct from the first—sometimes years after the first—a *second conversion,* as it is called."[12] By the first experience Boardman meant justification before God. By the second, he meant sanctification before men through which the sinner is made "holy in heart and life."[13]

Coming into existence in America, the second-blessing holiness concept of Christianity spread to England and Germany in the last quarter of the nineteenth century. It furnished the spiritual soil out of which the Pentecostal movement was born around the turn of the century. Charles Conn, the Pentecostal historian, calls the Pentecostal movement "an extension of the holiness revival" and declares that "most of those who received the Holy Ghost baptism during the earliest years were either those who were connected with the holiness revival or held holiness views."[14]

3. *Pentecostalism gained support and the cloak of doctrinal respectability as the result of the unprecise teaching concerning the Holy Spirit of a number of prominent Evangelicals of the late nineteenth and early twentieth century.*

These widely respected leaders, apparently influenced by the nineteenth-century holiness theology with its lack of doctrinal precision, taught the later distinctively Pentecostal tenet of the baptism of the Spirit as an experience subsequent to salvation. Foremost among these conservatives were F. B. Meyer, A. J. Gordon, A. B. Simpson, Andrew Murray, and most significant of all, R. A. Torrey.

Torrey may be said to be the one non-Pentecostal leader who, after Wesley and Finney, was the most influential in the prehistory of Pentecostalism. He gave the greatest impetus to the establishment of the movement as doctrinally respectable and experientially sound.

Although all of the evangelicals contemporary with the rise of Pentecostalism, who taught second-experience theology, constitute a kind of theological reservoir from which Pentecostals have drawn heavily to establish their central tenet of the baptism of the Spirit, none is quoted more frequently or more approvingly than R. A. Torrey, a non-Pentecostal.

The statement of Torrey most often quoted by Pentecostals to bolster their position on the baptism of the Spirit claims that regeneration by the Spirit and baptism with the Spirit do not occur at the same time. "The baptism of the Holy Spirit is an operation of the Holy Spirit distinct from and subsequent and additional to His regenerating work."[15]

Torrey's contention, much quoted by Pentecostals, continues by declaring, "A man may be regenerated by the Holy Spirit and still not be baptized with the Holy Spirit. . . . Every true believer has the Holy Spirit. But not every believer has the Baptism with the Holy Spirit, though every believer . . . may have."[16]

It is ironical, however, that what Pentecostal writers quote most frequently from Torrey represents an otherwise sound and incisive thinker and Bible teacher at his worst and not at his best—at his weakest and not at his strongest point. What is even more lamentable is that the halo of a great teacher's reputation for evangelical loyalty should be prostituted to invest a particular error he happened to fall into with the aura of truth and sound doctrine.

4. *Pentecostalism enjoyed great growth and expansion in the first half of the twentieth century.*

What came to be known as Pentecostalism arose among Christians, who according to Pentecostals were hungry for something more than they were getting in the average church. This "more" came in the form of speaking in tongues. When this phenomenon was connected with the conviction that speaking in another language was the evidence of the baptism of the Holy Spirit, the germinal idea of Pentecostal conviction was born. This occurred around the beginning of the twentieth century.

An outburst of tongues took place in Topeka, Kansas, in 1901, then sporadically around the world. In 1906 there was a startling manifestation of the charism at Azusa Street in Los Angeles, California. T. B. Barrett, a Norwegian Methodist pastor, who at the time was visiting America, received his "baptism" and returned to establish Pentecostalism in Norway, then in England, Germany, and Sweden.[17]

During the following years, Pentecostalism spread widely. Many groups came into being, some without the Pentecostal name, such as the Churches of God, International Church of the Foursquare Gospel, and the Catholic Apostolic Church. Others bore the Pentecostal name.

The largest and finest of Pentecostal groups that developed in the United States is the Assemblies of God. It was formed at Hot Springs, Arkansas, in 1914 by the merger of several Church of God congregations. In 1916 its headquarters was moved to Springfield, Missouri, where it has established a training school and a publishing house. "This is the only Pentecostal body," according to Elmer Clark, "which does not insist that sanctification is accomplished by a distinct work of grace subsequent to justification."[18] By 1950 it had grown to a sizeable denomination with some five thousand churches and about a quarter-million adherents.

Another group is the Pentecostal Holiness Church. It was organized at Clinton, North Carolina, in 1899. In 1911 it merged with the Fire-Baptized Holiness Church and has its headquarters at Franklin Springs, Georgia. By the middle of the century it had grown to more than 780 congregations and 26,000 members.

The United Pentecostal Church was formed in 1945 as the result of a merger with two other Pentecostal bodies. By mid-century it had approximately 1,000 churches and about 20,000 members.

Other Pentecostal bodies include the International Pentecostal Assemblies, the Pentecostal Church of God in America, the Pentecostal Fire-Baptized Holiness Church, Calvary Pentecostal Church, and the Pentecostal Assemblies of the World.

5. *Neo-Pentecostalism since its appearance about the middle of the twentieth century has been gradually assuming the designation of "The Charismatic Movement."*

In the early 1950's a new development began taking place in Pentecostalism. The Pentecostal blessing of the baptism of the Holy Spirit and tongues began to overleap the old-line Pentecostal denominations and to spread to non-Pentecostal churches, embracing practically all Protestant groups, and later invading even the Catholic church.[19]

These converts to Pentecostalism outside Pentecostal churches have been frequently called Neo-Pentecostals. The Neo-Pentecostal movement, moreover, has gradually been assuming the designation *charismatic.*[20] The usage, although popular, is misleading. It seems to infer that non-Pentecostal churches which do not practice the extraordinary or spectacular gifts featured in Pentecostal meetings (like speaking in tongues and healing) are not charismatic.

New Testament charismata (gift manifestations of the Holy Spirit) embrace far more gifts than just the spectacular ones. As Anthony Hoekema aptly observes: "Every Christian has gifts which are important for the body of believers. The term *charismatic,* therefore, ought not to be applied only to the Pentecostal or Neo-Pentecostal movement; the entire church of Jesus Christ is charismatic."[21]

The term *charismatic,* moreover, is misleading also in that while it avoids the connotations of emotional excitement and sometimes even frenzy occasionally connected with old-line Pentecostalism, it still stands for the same experience of so-called Spirit baptism and evidential tongues-speaking.

The rise of Neo-Pentecostalism can be traced to a number of causes. Chief among these is the spiritual deadness of the churches. Appealing to the doctrinally and spiritually malnourished among both Protestant and Catholic clergy and laity, Neo-Pentecostalism has promised a way to joy and power in life and service. Neo-Pentecostal Christians, like their older Pentecostal brothers, contend that this renewal is found in the long-neglected but now discovered and experienced baptism of the Holy Spirit with charismatic evidence of glossolalia.[22]

Where the church comprehends the glorious simplicity of the gospel and the completeness and fulness of the salvation it brings the moment faith is exercised in Christ Jesus the Saviour, the appeal of Neo-Pentecostalism will be nil. When the Word of God is given preeminence and sound Bible doctrine, especially in the sphere of the theology of the Holy Spirit, is stressed and made the test of experience, the claims of charismatic Christianity will be rejected.[23]

But wherever a believer fails to see his position in Christ and loses sight of the complete adequacy of his resources in that position, Pentecostalism will appear on the scene with large advantages. But when Christians see what they are in Christ and begin to claim the glory of that position in their daily experience, the appeal of Pentecostalism and its doctrine of a second experience will vanish.

In the place of a second experience will come an unbroken chain of thrilling experiences that will continue and grow in power and intensity as faith is reposed in the believer's position in Christ and step by step the blessing of that position is appropriated by faith. Then and *only then* will the Saviour's words be realized. "He who believes in Me, as the Scripture said, 'From his innermost being shall flow rivers of living water' " (Jn 7:38, NASV).

THE BAPTISM OF THE SPIRIT IN CHARISMATIC CHRISTIANITY

1. *The belief that the baptism of the Spirit is subsequent to salvation is the basic tenet of charismatic Christianity.*

The Pentecostal concept of the baptism of the Spirit centers in the experience of the Holy Spirit. This is specifically a post-regeneration *filling* of the Spirit, evidenced initially by charismatic tongues-speaking and made possible by meeting the conditions of faith and complete obedience.

It is quite obvious to the careful Bible student that this view of the baptism of the Spirit is based upon experience rather than doctrine. This does not mean that Pentecostals do not have a doctrine of the baptism of the Spirit. It does mean, however, that their doctrine on this vital subject, although based upon the Bible, is not *soundly* biblical.

The reason is quite obvious. Pentecostals build their doctrine of Spirit-baptism only upon part of the relevant Biblical evidence rather than upon the full testimony of Scripture. Moreover, their interpretation of this partial evidence, almost exclusively the book of Acts, is faulty because it erects its teaching on these historical and experiential portions, at the same time construing them in a time vacuum and failing to reconcile their conclusions with the great doctrinal epistles of the New Testament.[24]

Doctrinal ambiguity concerning the baptism of the Spirit, as has been noted in previous pages, has been inherited by charismatic Christianity from its forbears in early Wesleyan second-experience perfectionism, Finney's theology of revivalism, the second-blessing teaching of the holiness movement, and the Pentecostal movement itself, born from these preceding movements, at the beginning of the twentieth century.

Pentecostals frequently use the ambiguous term *full gospel.** Under this designation they include a number of doctrines and experiences, such as conversion, sanctification, evangelism, healing, and the second advent. But no other doctrine or experience has the unanimous voice or cohesive power in Pentecostalism as the so-called baptism of the Holy Spirit as recorded in Acts 2:4.

Pentecostals themselves confess that the only area of theology in which Pentecostalism is distinctive is pneumatology, and that only in one particular phase of the Spirit's work. Pentecostals hold that subsequent to conversion there is a spiritual baptism of power, evidenced by glossolalia, as at Pentecost.[25] This is the criterion that differentiates Pentecostals from all other evangelical, fundamental, and holiness groups.[26]

By the literature and testimony of Pentecostalism, it is patent that the baptism of the Spirit and the resultant charismata, notably tongues, constitute the Pentecostal distinctive. Doctrines and experiences outside this thematic center are peripheral and for all practical purposes undeveloped in Pentecostalism.

2. *Charismatic Christianity's basic tenet of a post-conversion baptism of the Spirit requires subscribing to two spiritual baptisms.*

This is inevitable because the clear teaching of the apostle Paul is that *every* believer, the moment he is saved, is baptized

---

*This usage is unhappy inasmuch as there is only one true gospel. Any other gospel is a false gospel (Gal 1:6-9). The gospel does not admit of the epithet "full" or "non-full," but only true or false. Moreover, the true gospel brings salvation, which is always "full," never partial or piecemeal and identical in content for all believers. Hence it is a common salvation, based on what Christ has done for us and what we are in Him, not what we have done for God or are in ourselves.

into Christ—"in the sphere of" (locative *en*) or "by" the Spirit as instrument or agency (1 Co 12:13). Hence baptism *in the sphere* of the Spirit is Spirit-baptism, whether one construes the Greek preposition *en* as locative or instrumental.

In the face of this plain declaration concerning Spirit baptism, charismatic theology is forced to posit *two* spiritual baptisms. It declares that while every Christian has been baptized into Christ, not every Christian has yet been baptized *by Christ* (as agent) *in* the Spirit as an element.

In other words the charismatic belief is that while the Spirit has baptized every believer into Christ (conversion), Christ has not yet baptized every believer into the Spirit (Pentecost baptism).[27]

In the Pentecostal position it is plain that two spiritual baptisms are subscribed to—one into Christ at regeneration, one into the Holy Spirit as a subsequent experience. This contention, however, must be made in contradiction of the apostle Paul's clear declaration that there is only *one spiritual* baptism for this age (Eph 4:5), and that this is the baptism that places *all* believers in Christ, and hence constitutes not a second experience for some believers, but an inseparable part of salvation enjoyed by *all* believers (1 Co 12:13)!

In addition, in construing the baptism of the Spirit as a second experience after salvation, Pentecostals must face not only the complete absence of any evidence in the New Testament epistles to support such a second spiritual baptism, but the overwhelming evidence of the doctrinal portions against it.

More serious still, the Pentecostal interpretation of the book of Acts, from which Pentecostals almost completely draw their second-experience view of Spirit-baptism, is strongly suspect for a number of reasons. In the first place it fails to take into account the nondoctrinal and purely historical and experiential nature of the book of Acts. Moreover, it interprets the pivotal passages allegedly teaching a second spiritual baptism (Ac 2:4; 8:14-16; 10:34-36; 19:1-7) in a *time vacuum*, failing to see the inaugural features of a new age being intro-

-duced and to differentiate these from the noninaugural features once the age was established.

In the third place the Pentecostal interpretation of Acts is made also in a theological and doctrinal vacuum as well as a time vacuum. A second spiritual baptism after regeneration simply does not square with the rest of the Word of God, sound historical evangelical theology or the witness of Church history.

3. *The belief that speaking in a supernatural language is the initial evidence of the baptism of the Spirit is the unique emphasis of charismatic Christianity.*

As the Pentecostalist Donald Gee declares, "The distinctive doctrine of the Pentecostal churches is that speaking with tongues is the 'initial evidence' of the baptism in the Holy Spirit. This article of belief is now incorporated in the official doctrinal schedules of practically all Pentecostal denominations."[28]

Pentecostalism inherited the idea of the baptism of the Holy Spirit as a critically important spiritual experience beyond regeneration from classic Methodism, Finney revivalism, and the holiness movement. Moreover, this conviction it shares with many in conservative evangelicalism. The unique feature of Pentecostalism is the claim that speaking in tongues as at Pentecost is the initial evidence of this spiritual baptism. This distinguishes its proponents as Pentecostal. It is not far amiss to say that the idea of combining tongues with the holiness idea of the baptism of the Spirit was the catalyst that generated the Pentecostal movement.

In tongues-speaking, old-line Pentecostalism felt it had found an objective criterion to remove the ambiguity of feeling and the subjective evidence Wesley and his holiness followers had relied upon to give assurance they had received the second blessing or perfection experience they advocated.

But the question may be asked, What about the attitude of Neo-Pentecostals toward the old-line Pentecostal claim that tongues is the indispensable evidence of having received "the baptism of the Spirit"? The answer is that some do continue to make the claim. Howard M. Ervin, a recent Neo-Pentecostal writer, makes tongues the "external and indubitable proof" of Spirit-baptism.[29]

Other Neo-Pentecostals, however, do not insist that speaking in tongues is the indispensable sign and that one may receive this baptism apart from actual glossalalic manifestation.[30] Yet even those in the latter category regard speaking with tongues as highly desirable evidence of Spirit baptism, giving it "an objectivity" that has "a definite value for one's continued walk in the Spirit."[31] Kevin and Dorothy Ranaghan are "convinced that as far as the Charismatic movement is concerned, everyone touched by it is meant to pray in tongues, that in fact, the gift of tongues is always given by the Lord as he renews the life of the Spirit."[32] These same writers declare tongues to be "a normal and usual result of the baptism in the Holy Spirit" from Pentecost onward and urge believers to pray for and expect the manifestation.[33]

4. *The belief prevails in charismatic Christianity that certain conditions must precede the baptism of the Spirit.*

Conversion or regeneration is posited as the indispensable pre-condition for the Penecostal baptism, for it is considered a second experience after salvation. Obedience must also be exercised, to be followed by faith. The faith which Pentecostalism requires is apparently not identical with saving faith in Christ, but sanctifying faith directed toward the Holy Spirit.

The confusion that prevails in Pentecostalism concerning conditions for Spirit-baptism is the result of confounding the baptism of the Spirit with the filling of the Spirit. Actually the baptism of the Spirit is not a second experience after salvation at all but a vital and inseparable part of salvation—the result of simple faith in Christ's redemptive grace—a position before God rather than an experience. The experience of that position of being "in Christ" as a result of the Spirit's work in baptism is the filling of the Spirit.

It is the filling of the Spirit, based upon positional fullness secured by our great salvation, that is to be a continuous and ever-expanding experience of the Christian life. This experience of the filling of the Spirit, moreover, is *on the same basis* of simple faith as salvation itself. It could not be otherwise because it is a vital and inseparable part of that salvation, *not* something in addition to it.

So-called conditions for the experience of the infilling (such as separation from sin, surrender to God's will, etc.) are not separate conditions at all. They are rather *manifestations* of enlightened faith, which reckons on what we are in Christ and what He had done for us. This contrasts with unenlightened faith which trusts rather in what we can do for Christ and what we are in ourselves.

It is the widespread confusion occasioned by the charismatic movements of our times that calls for clarification of what the baptism of the Holy Spirit is and does in the life of the believer. Only a careful study of the Scripture witness on this subject can remove the scales from men's eyes that are causing them to wander in the quagmire of experiences not really authenticated by the Word of God. Only a return to what the Bible teaches concerning the baptism of the Spirit can restore the vision of God's people to comprehend what they are in Christ and how big their salvation in Him is.

Only this vision will rescue believers from the snare of seeking some experience outside of and in addition to that "so great salvation" (Heb 2:3), purchased by our Saviour at Calvary and inwrought in the believer by the Holy Spirit the moment faith is reposed in Christ's completed redemptive work. To be safeguarded in doctrine as well as life, every believer must see that each infilling of the Spirit, the second as well as each succeeding infilling, is not something in addition to salvation, but a glorious realization and appropriation of the great gift of salvation itself.[34]

2

The Baptism of the Spirit Misunderstood

THE BAPTISM of the Holy Spirit is one of the most vital and important scriptural doctrines. The baptism is that divine operation of God's Spirit which places the believer in Christ, in His mystical body, the church, and which makes him one with all other believers in Christ. The baptism makes them one in the life of the Son of God Himself, sharing His common salvation, hope, and destiny. Thus, this major Bible theme concerns intimately and vitally the believer's position and experience, his standing and state.

It is astonishing, however, that a subject of such importance should suffer from both its enemies and friends. From its enemies the doctrine has suffered not so much from hostility or opposition as from neglect. It is simply ignored or treated superficially. Those who reject dispensational teaching and posit an all-time grace covenant, who make no adequate distinction between the assembly of Israel in the wilderness in the Old Testament and the church as the body of Christ in the New Testament, simply do not know what to do with it. To them it remains a scriptural riddle.

This doctrine has especially been wounded in the house of its friends. Large groups of well-meaning but poorly-taught Christians, in reaction against the neglect of this doctrine, have taken it to heart, according it great prominence. In their zeal, however, they have not always confined themselves to accurate scriptural statement.

Indeed, it would be difficult to find a biblical theme more

used to teach deeper spiritual living and yet at the same time subject to more misconception, misstatement, and confusion, than this one. Nowhere in biblical theology is there greater need for precise statement of vital truth than with the doctrine of the baptism of the Spirit. But what are the reasons for misconception and misstatement? Where does the confusion arise? These questions are pertinent and touch at the heart of the matter.

WHAT THE BAPTISM OF THE HOLY SPIRIT IS NOT

1. The baptism of the Spirit is not the new birth.

Although in this present age of grace regeneration and the baptism with the Spirit are always simultaneous—so that everyone who is regenerated is at the same time baptized by the Spirit into the body of Christ—yet the two operations are distinct. They must not be confused as one operation. G. Campbell Morgan fails to make the necessary distinction when he writes: "The baptism of the Spirit is the primary blessing; it is, in short, the blessing of regeneration."[1]

However, a careful consideration will show that the baptism with the Holy Spirit is *not* regeneration. The Spirit's baptizing work places the believer in Christ (Ro 6:3, 4; Gal 3:27; 1 Co 12:13; Col 2:12), whereas regeneration results in Christ in the believer (Jn 17:23; Col 1:27; Rev 3:20). Regeneration imparts life. The baptism with the Spirit unites the life-possessing one to Christ, and to those who possess life in Him. Did not Jesus, in His great upper room discourse, when uttering words prophetic of the Spirit's advent into the world at Pentecost, and His ministry during this present age, refer to a distinction between these two operations of the Spirit as "ye in me" and "I in you" (Jn 14:20)?

That the expression *ye in me* plainly refers to the Spirit's baptizing the believer into Christ is evident from Galatians 3:27, "For as many of you as have been baptized into Christ have put on Christ"; and from 1 Corinthians 12:13, "For by one Spirit are we all baptized into one body." There are, moreover, approximately 150 passages which state or imply that the believer is in Christ, and every one has reference to the Spirit's work in baptism, for that operation alone can put one in Christ.

That the phrase *I in you* refers to regeneration is apparent from 1 John 5:11, 12: "And this is the record, that God hath given to us eternal life, and this life is in his Son. He that hath the Son hath life, and he that hath not the Son of God hath not life." Regeneration means receiving spiritual life, that is, eternal life. Christ is this life (Jn 14:6). We only receive this life as we receive Christ, who then may be said to be in us, "the hope of glory" (Col 1:27).

The baptism with the Holy Spirit and regeneration are thus two complementary and yet distinct works of God, simultaneously and eternally accomplished in the believer the moment he exercises saving faith in Christ. By regeneration the soul is quickened from death into life (Eph 2:1-5). By the Spirit's baptizing work the quickened soul is organically united to Christ as head (Eph 1:22, 23) and to all other believers as members of the one body (1 Co 12:12-27). By regeneration the one exercising saving faith becomes a child of God (Jn 1:12, 13), is made a son in the Father's house (Gal 3:26), becomes a partaker of the divine nature (2 Pe 1:4), and is made an heir of God and a joint-heir with Christ (Ro 8:16, 17). By the Spirit's baptizing work, the believing one is taken out of the old creation in Adam and placed eternally in the new creation in Christ (2 Co 5:17), the new federal head, and all that Christ is and has done is imputed to the believer. Our Saviour, in His words, "ye in me, and I in you," inseparably connects these two operations of the Spirit in this age but also carefully distinguishes them.

2. *The baptism of the Spirit is not the indwelling of the Spirit.*

The uniform teaching of the epistles is that every believer in this age has the Spirit (Ro 5:5; 8:9; Gal 3:2; 4:6) and is indwelt continually by the Spirit (1 Co 6:19, 20; Ro 8:11; 2 Co 5:5; 1 Jn 3:24; 4:13). The difference between the saved of this age and the unsaved is that all the saved have the Spirit indwelling them, while all the unsaved "have not the Spirit" (Jude 19). Like regeneration, the indwelling with the Spirit during this age occurs simultaneously with the baptism with the Spirit and yet is a distinct ministry of the Spirit. It is impossible now to be regenerated and not to be indwelt with the Spirit nor baptized with the Spirit. This ought not to surprise anyone who has given any serious thought to the breadth and complexity of that great work of God for the believer, which is described by the very general term *salvation*. This is the great inclusive word of the gospel and embraces the sweep of divine undertakings from our redemption from sin in the past to our complete glorification in the future.

The late Lewis Sperry Chafer lists some thirty-three distinct positions and possessions into which one who is saved is ushered the very moment he exercises faith.[2] Regeneration, baptism, and indwelling are accomplished for the believer at the instant he believes. They form the structure of his salvation and are never annulled; thus they never need to be repeated.

3. *The baptism of the Spirit is not the sealing of the Spirit.*

The sealing is a distinct operation of the Spirit but occurs simultaneously with regeneration, baptism, and indwelling. Every child of God has been sealed with the Spirit unto the time of full redemption and glorification of the body (Eph 1:13; 4:30; 2 Co 1:22), and also anointed with the Spirit (2 Co 1:21; 1 Jn 2:20, 27). The Spirit, as the indweller, is the seal. The figure of the seal speaks of the stamp of the divine ownership as a result of the new creation in Christ Jesus, and it is the badge of eternal security. Those whom God stamps as His own, He pledges to keep as His own.

By regeneration He gives us His own life. By the Spirit's baptism He unites us indissolubly and vitally to Himself. By the indwelling He grants us His continual presence. By the sealing He stamps us as His very own for all eternity. By the anointing He consecrates us to a holy life and service. God's work is always perfect and complete.

4. *The baptism of the Spirit is not a second blessing.*

Many modern holiness movements and old-line Pentecostals from 1900 on and Neo-Pentecostals since 1950 are guilty of this fatal blunder. Absolutely essential time distinctions are completely ignored and are even looked upon hostilely as subtle human reasonings and positive Satanic inventions to shut out the power of God. The baptism of Jesus is distorted to teach a second definite experience in the life of our Saviour, a so-called baptism of Christ's human nature with the Holy Spirit before entering upon His ministry. The transitional nature of the period in which the apostles lived is completely disregarded, and they are viewed as regenerated before Pentecost, and what happened on that day is explained as a second experience, the baptism with the Holy Spirit.

The confusion proceeds. The Samaritan disciples (Ac 8) are regarded as regenerated under Philip's preaching, and later baptized with the Holy Spirit as a second definite experience under Peter and John's ministry. Paul is said to have been regenerated on the road to Damascus, and subsequently baptized with the Spirit as a second definite experience when Ananias laid his hands on him, and he was filled with the Spirit (Ac 9). Likewise Cornelius is strangely represented as saved before Peter's arrival (but see Ac 11:14) and baptized with the Spirit as a second experience in the course of Peter's sermon (Ac 10). In like manner the Ephesian disciples (Ac 19) are confidently affirmed to have been genuine New Testament believers before they met Paul, and their receiving the Holy Spirit was their baptism with the Spirit as a second definite experience. Deeper experiences of famous Christians down through the centuries are misconstrued as second definite experiences after regeneration.[3]

In many instances promoters of these unsound doctrines make no attempt to reconcile their teaching of a second definite experience gleaned from the gospels and the Acts with the clear-cut teaching of the epistles, namely, that all believers in this age have the Holy Spirit and are regenerated, baptized, indwelt, anointed, and sealed as God's own forever, the moment saving faith is exercised.

Some, making a serious effort to interpret Acts in the light of the doctrinal epistles, teach that 1 Corinthians 12:13 is a so-called baptism of repentance, which results in salvation in distinction to the baptism with the Holy Spirit, a subsequent experience for power.[4] Thus two spiritual baptisms are posited for this age, and this in the face of Paul's emphatic testimony, "one [spiritual] baptism" (Eph 4:5).

Others, comparing the doctrine of the epistles with the historical portions, cannot get beyond the erroneous notion of "two classes of passages" in the former, which are accordingly twisted to fit the mold of error, drawn out of an inaccurate and nondispensational interpretation of the latter.[5] Yet others, teaching that a person may or may not be baptized with the Spirit "the moment he is regenerated," apparently do not realize how contrary such a position is to the epistles.[6]

Misunderstanding of Spirit baptism has led multitudes of present-day believers to great lengths. This is especially so since 1950 when Pentecostal revivalism began to overflow the confines of old-line Pentecostalism and, in the Neo-Pentecostal movement, began to inundate practically all Protestant denominations and Roman Catholicism.[7]

As a result, confusion is widespread. Christians are urged to seek the Holy Spirit, to tarry for their Pentecost. One group preaches to believers a twofold step to the Spirit's baptism. First, a step of entire surrender. Second, a definite reception of the Holy Spirit "by faith." Another denomination insists on a supernatural speaking in tongues as the evidence of what they call the baptism with the Spirit.[8] Another large group considers speaking in a charismatic language as the evidence of the new birth, which is made synonymous with the baptism with the Spirit.

Other groups interpret the baptizing work of the Holy Spirit as an experience of perfect holiness, and fall into the mistaken notion of sinless perfection and eradicationism. All—in viewing the Spirit's baptizing work as a second blessing or second work of grace for the believer—necessarily cast a reflection on the completeness of the first work of grace, in which Christ, in all His fullness, becomes the portion of the believer the moment he is saved. A great barrier is erected against the glorious truth of the safety and security of the believer the instant the scriptural truth of the baptism with the Spirit is distorted or mutilated. This is obvious since the Scriptures represent us as in Christ, in indissoluble and eternal union, by the Spirit's baptizing work.

5. *The baptism of the Spirit is not the filling of the Spirit.*

It is a common practice among Pentecostals and Neo-Pentecostals to identify the baptism of the Spirit with the filling of the Spirit. "To be Pentecostal," declares Ernest Williams, "is to identify oneself with the experience that came to Christ's followers on the day of Pentecost, that is, to be filled with the Holy Spirit in the same manner as those who were filled with the Holy Spirit on that occasion."[9]

That the two operations of the Spirit, so frequently confounded, are not the same is evident from a number of emphatic scriptural contrasts.

First, the baptizing work of the Spirit is a once-for-all operation, whereas the filling with the Spirit is a continuous process.

One baptism for the believer is in contrast to the many infillings. The one baptism puts the believer "in Christ" (Ro 6:3, 4; Gal 3:27; Col 2:12), into His body (1 Co 12:13), and therefore brings the believing one into an eternal position, which is unalterable and immutable, having the finality of God's own unchangeable nature, of which the believer becomes partaker (2 Pe 1:4). Since this position in Christ is unchangeable and eternal, the baptizing work of the Spirit is not repeatable, as there is not the least occasion for its being repeated. One in Christ positionally can never again through all eternity be out of Christ positionally, as that position depends wholly upon the efficacy of the finished redemptive work of God's Son, and does not hinge upon human merit or faithfulness. Accordingly, the baptism with the Spirit is never said to be repeated, nor indeed can be. However, it does effect positional fullness, the completeness with which God views the believer, because it places the believer in Christ, in whom all fullness dwells (Col 2:9-10). As a result, the believer shares that spiritual fullness and is complete in Christ when saved.

Nonexperiential (positional) fullness, moreover, is the ground of experiential fullness, which is the actual repeatable filling with the Spirit (Ac 2:4; 4:8, 31; 9:17). By faith the believer reckons on his positional fullness as his heritage in union with Christ. As he believes he is what he is in Christ, his position becomes real in his experience (Ro 6:11).

Accordingly, the baptism of the Spirit effects union with Christ and positional fullness. It makes possible the filling, but emphatically it is not the experience of the filling itself.

The baptizing work of the Spirit is nonexperiential, whereas the filling with the Spirit is experiential.

The baptism with the Spirit is not an experience. It does not affect the believer's senses. Like the spiritual (positional) fullness it effects by bringing the believer into the sphere of spiritual blessing, it is not felt. Placing the believer in Christ, it constitutes his initiation into the Christian life but plays no part in his subsequent experience, except as it forms the basis of his experience of his exalted position in Christ (Eph 1:3).

The filling with the Spirit, in contrast to the baptism of the Spirit, is a very definite experience. It radically affects Christian life and service. It produces Christian character in the ninefold fruit of the Spirit (Gal 5:22, 23). It produces power for testimony (Ac 1:8), boldness for witnessing (Ac 4:31), victory over the flesh (Gal 5:16), exercise of gifts (1 Co 12:4-31). It results in the Spirit's teaching (Jn 16:13; 1 Jn 2:27), true praise and worship (Eph 5:18-20), guidance (Ro 8:14), effective prayer (Ro 8:27), etc. The filling with the Spirit produces normal Christian experience; and continual filling is necessary to maintain the norm.

There is no command for anyone to be baptized with the Spirit, but there is a distinct injunction for every believer to be filled with the Spirit. The unequivocal declaration of Scripture (1 Co 12:13) is that all believers "were baptized by one Spirit into one body." No command appears for the simple reason that it is an absolute impossibility to be a Christian at all in this age and not be baptized with the Spirit! The admonition to be filled continually is outspoken and emphatic. "And be not drunk with wine, wherein is excess; but be filled with the Spirit" (Eph 5:18). These words also indicate that it is possible for a believer *not* to be filled.

The present tense of the verb in the imperative denotes a "continuous or repeated" action so that the meaning is "keep on being filled," or "be constantly filled."[10] Thus is expressed the constant duty and obligation of the believer and thus is emphasized the contrast between the once-for-all nature of the Spirit's work in baptizing, and the continuous and oft-recurring nature of His work in filling.

The baptizing work of the Spirit is universal among Christians, whereas the filling with the Spirit is not. All Christians are so baptized, without a single exception (1 Co 12:13), even the carnal or fleshly, and the babes in Christ (1 Co 3:1-3), even those who may have fallen into sin (1 Co 5:1-10), and all so baptized are thereby positionally justified and sanctified (1 Co 1:2; 6:11), being "saints" (1 Co 1:2). That all are not filled with the Spirit is obvious from the carnal state of the Corinthian believers, who are "all" yet said to have been baptized with the Spirit. It may then be said that all Christians are baptized with the Spirit, but all are not filled, although all ought to be filled, and that constantly.

Believers who habitually live the Spirit-filled life are described as "full" (an adjective) of the Holy Spirit (Ac 6:3; 7:55; 11:24). When the precise action of infilling is in view, the verb is used (Ac 2:4; 4:8, 31; 9:17; 13:9, 52; Eph 5:18).

The baptizing work of the Spirit is totally different from the filling with the Spirit in its results. Being nonexperiential, as noted, as over against the filling, which is experiential, it concerns the standing or position of the believer, whereas the filling concerns his state or walk. It results, accordingly, in the believer's exalted standing before God, which is the result of the work of Christ, and is perfect and entire from the very moment saving faith is exercised in Christ. Nothing in the subsequent life of the believer can ever, even in the smallest degree, add to, or subtract from his title to God's favor, nor to his perfect security.

The baptizing work of the Spirit, putting the believing one in Christ, alone confers standing in God's sight, and gives the weakest, most ignorant man on earth, the moment he believes, the same position as the most illustrious saint (Jn 1:12; Ro

8:17; Eph 1:6, 11; 2:4-6; 5:30; 1 Pe 1:4, 5; Col 2:10). What the actual state of such a one may be, is quite a different matter. Certainly it must be thought of as far below his exalted standing before God.

It is by the filling with the Spirit that the believer is enabled to maintain a state worthy of his standing (Eph 4:1-3; Ro 12:3-21). Positional sanctification, which is the result of the Spirit's baptizing work, is accompanied by progressive or experiential sanctification, as a result of the Spirit's work in filling. As C. I. Scofield aptly remarks: "The divine order, under grace, is first to give the highest possible standing, and then to exhort the believer to maintain a state in accordance therewith. The beggar is lifted up from the dunghill and set among princes (I Sam. 2:8), and then exhorted to be princely."[11]

It is to be noted that not only the baptizing work of the Spirit, but His regenerating, indwelling, and sealing are included under the term *gift* or *free gift* of the Holy Spirit (Ac 2:38). The salvation which He works in us is also said to be a free gift (Eph 2:8-10), a gift of grace, (Ro 6:23), that is, "a favor which one receives without any merit of his own."[12] Thus the baptizing work of the Spirit with the spiritual fullness it effects by placing *all* believers "in Christ" is associated with God's free gift of salvation. The filling with the Spirit, on the other hand, while based on spiritual fullness provided in salvation, is to be connected with rewards, which are to be given to believers for faithfulness in service *after* receiving God's free gift of salvation (1 Co 3:10-15; 2 Co 5:10; 2 Jn 8).

In proportion as the believer walks by means of the Spirit (Gal 5:16), being continually filled with the Spirit (Eph 5:18), will he be enabled to fulfill all God's plan for his life, in carrying out the program of good works for which he is saved (Eph 2:10), and thus receive a full reward (2 Jn 8).

The baptizing work of the Spirit is different from the filling with the Spirit in the conditions upon which it is received. Since it is a vital and integral part of salvation, together with the spiritual fullness it effects in Christ, simple faith in Christ as Saviour from the penalty of sin is the only requirement. "Believe on the Lord Jesus Christ, and thou shalt be saved" (Ac

16:31). "Whosoever believeth on him shall not perish, but have everlasting life" (Jn 3:16).

But the filling of the Spirit is also the experience and the expression of salvation, *not* something in addition to it. Hence, actually from the divine side, the filling, like the baptism, has only *one* condition—that of simple faith. However, the faith is not that of the unsaved person believing that Christ died for him. It is by contrast the faith of the saint (the saved person) believing that he died in Christ—died to sin and self (Ro 5:6-8) that he might live unto God and righteousness (Ro 6:1-11).

The New Testament bears clear testimony that being filled with the Spirit is *not* a matter of legalistically meeting certain human prerequisites such as yieldedness (Ro 6:13, 19; 12:1-2), confession of (1 Jn 1:9) and separation from sin (2 Co 6:1-2). These and other so-called conditons (made so much of in charismatic circles[13]) are valid *only* as expressions of faith in what Christ has done for us and what we are in Him. Never are they valid as works we do for God to merit His great salvation, or *any* experience or expression of it.

6. *The baptism of the Spirit is not water baptism.*

One extreme position erroneously views Spirit baptism as a once-for-all operation at Pentecost (Acts 2) and in Cornelius' house (Acts 10), and maintains that then it ceased. During this present age, it is contended, there is no baptism with the Holy Spirit. First Corinthians 12:13 is construed as referring back to these events. Such scriptures as Romans 6:3, 4; Colossians 2:12; Galatians 3:27; 1 Peter 3:21, are made to refer exclusively to water baptism. The "one baptism" of Ephesians 4:5 is also asserted to be water baptism alone.

I. M. Haldeman, adopting this position, comments thus on Ephesians 4:5:

> If it be Holy Ghost baptism, water baptism is excluded. There is no authority, no place for it. No minister has a right to perform it; no one is under obligation to submit to it. To perform it, or submit to it, would be not only without au-

thority, but useless, utterly meaningless. If it be water baptism, Holy Ghost baptism is no longer operative. Baptism
must be either the one or the other, Holy Ghost or water. It
cannot be both. Two are no longer permissible.[14]

Others adopting the opposite extreme position, while rightly
insisting that Ephesians 4:5 refers to Spirit baptism, drastically
rule out any practice of water baptism for the church age. Although they find ritual baptism, of course, regularly practiced
in the early church (Ac 2:38; 8:12, 13, 16, 36; 9:18; 10:47,
48; 16:15, 33; 18:8; 19:3-5) and mentioned in 1 Corinthians
1:13-17, this practice is thought to be confined to the early
so-called Jewish church, and discontinued by the apostle Paul,
when the alleged "real" New Testament church began late in
the book of Acts.

This position must be rejected. The basic fact, which is
ignored, is that the church actually began with the baptizing
work of the Holy Spirit on the day of Pentecost (Ac 1:4, 5;
2:47, with 11:16; 1 Co 12:13), and that water baptism, which
in the new dispensation was to become the symbol of Spirit
baptism, was regularly administered, not only in the so-called
Jewish church, but also long after in fully established Gentile
churches (Ac 18:8; 1 Co 1:13-17).

It was fitting, too, that water baptism should become a visible
portrayal of that all-important invisible operation of the Holy
Spirit that places the believer in union with Christ (Ro 6:3, 4)
and with His body, the church (1 Co 12:13). It attached
unifying and instructive significance to the water ceremony
thus to focus its meaning upon the believer's oneness with his
Lord and with all other believers in Him. Water baptism could
be viewed as a visible symbol of the Holy Spirit's work of
baptizing the believer into Christ either as the *cause* or *means*
effecting that glorious union or as the *result* or *effect* of that
union in the believer's life.

In the former case the application of water by sprinkling or
pouring is viewed as the coming of the Holy Spirit upon the
recipient to effect His baptizing work. In the latter case the
immersion of the believer in water is interpreted as visibly
symbolizing the believer's union with Christ in death, burial,

and resurrection. This position views water baptism as only validly Christian when it is preceded by Spirit baptism.

The apostle, in speaking of the "one baptism" in Ephesians 4:5, is speaking of Spirit baptism, which is likewise the case in Romans 6:3, 4; Colossians 2:12; and Galatians 3:27. But when he describes this momentous operation of the Spirit as the one baptism and as one of the seven essential unities to be recognized and kept in maintaining Christian oneness and concord, he is certainly not implying that water baptism is no longer to be administered. He is merely saying, "There is only one [spiritual] baptism." Although his theme is no more water baptism in Romans 6:3, 4; Colossians 2:12; and Galatians 3:27 than in Ephesians 4:5, it must be remembered that in any reference to Spirit baptism the ritual symbol is *always* behind the spiritual reality, and these passages are no exception.

Therefore, although the apostle is not considering ritual but real baptism, the context of the argument and the exalted nature of the spiritual realities taught strongly supporting this view, nevertheless water baptism as a practice for this age cannot validly be said to be ruled out by these passages.

On the other hand, however, it is to be feared that man in displacing Spirit baptism by water baptism in these sublime passages has put them into ecclesiastical racks and tortured and twisted them until they have screamed out some confession never written in them. To be sure, this torturous process began very early, doubtless within the lifetime of the apostle, for man is always keenly tempted to substitute ritual for reality in things spiritual. But it is difficult to see how a first-century reader, especially one who had sat under the teaching of the great apostle of grace, had listened to his magnificent expositions of the believer's position of union with Christ by the Spirit's baptizing work and had noted his rigid practice of putting the ritual strictly in its proper place of subordination (1 Co 1:14-17), would have imagined that in these sublime Scriptures setting forth tremendous spiritual realities of the believer's in-Christ position Paul would be dealing with a mere ceremony.

It is difficult also on the basis of biblical, historical, and philological consideration to see how a first-century reader would have construed the baptism of Romans 6:3, 4; Colossians 2:12; Galatians 3:27; and Ephesians 4:5 as water baptism. Could a mere water ceremony affect the vast spiritual transaction comprehended in being placed "in Christ"? Valid Christian baptism (the water ceremony) performed upon a true believer can and does portray Spirit baptism, which has already taken place in the believer's life. But the ritual ceremony is only in the background, never in the foreground. It is the reality that is the subject of these passages, not the ritual symbolism that underlies it.

Many Christian scholars, however, are persuaded that a particular mode of baptism cannot be deduced from the terms *death, burial,* and *resurrection* contained in these passages. Baptism, referring to the Levitical ceremonies of the Old Testament (Heb 9:10), it is maintained, had come to have a wide meaning of "ceremonial cleansing, or ritual purification by water, and that by sprinkling or pouring," centuries before the Christian era.

Edmund Fairfield[15] illustrates this established biblical usage of the term *baptize* (*baptizo*) from the Septuagint, the Apocrypha, Josephus, and the Greek New Testament. James W. Dale has researched the subject of water baptism among the ancient Jews. He concludes his extensive researches with this summary statement: "Judaic baptism is a condition of Ceremonial Purification effected by washing . . . sprinkling . . . pouring . . . dependent in no wise on any form of act, or on the covering of the object."[16]

Dale summarizes his detailed work on the study of John the Baptist's baptism with these words: "This same *baptisma* is declared by word and exhibited in symbol, by the application of pure water to the person in the ritual ordinance. This is Johannic Baptism in its shadow. . . . Dipping or immersing in water is phraseology utterly unknown to John's baptism."[17]

Biblical, historical, and philological evidence, therefore, is not lacking that John the Baptist "ceremonially purified" (baptized) by sprinkling or pouring, that Jesus was so baptized (consecrated) to His priesthood (Ex 29:4; Ps 110:1; Mt 3:15;

Heb 7-9),[18] and that Jewish and Christian baptism knew no other mode.[19]

Whatever mode of baptism may be employed, however, let no one suppose because water baptism is not the apostle's subject in Romans 6:3-4; Colossians 2:12; Galatians 3:27, and Ephesians 4:5, except of course, as the symbol always underlies the reality, that therefore there is no longer any warrant for the practice of ritual baptism in the church age. With water baptism practiced in the early church, as noted, even to a late date among believers of purely Gentile background, to posit no water baptism for this dispensation on the basis of the "one baptism" of Ephesians 4:5 is an extreme position, unwarranted by all the facts of the case. That which is not the subject of this passage cannot be said to be eliminated by the scope of the passage. The apostle simply does not have ritual baptism in mind in these words, as the context plainly intimates, and hence they do not deal with the practice or nonpractice of the rite in this age.

WHAT MISUNDERSTANDING OF THE BAPTISM OF THE SPIRIT LEADS TO

This whole theme is far from being a mere discussion of words. It is a sad spectacle to see the widespread havoc wrought in the church of Christ the world over by miscomprehension of Spirit baptism. Confusion has steadily increased, especially since the rise of the neo-Pentecostal or charismatic trend since 1950. Crossing the confines of the older Pentecostal denominations, this trend has overflowed into practically every Protestant group and Roman Catholicism, furnishing the basis for new errors to trouble the peace and doctrinal purity of the church.[20] Destructive and dangerous results of this prevailing condition are not difficult to discover.

1. *This misunderstanding leads to divisions and lamentable confusion among God's people.*

Multitudes of believers seeking some experience not authorized by the Word of God have imagined themselves to have received some special benefit, some peculiar blessing, placing them above their brethren. Error has ministered to empty spiritual pride. Disruptions and separations have flourished like weeds in rank soil of spiritual arrogance. Churches have been split—believers divided.

The believer's union with Christ is obscured, as well as his oneness with *all* other believers in Christ. Instead of *one* body formed by *one* spiritual baptism (1 Co 12:13), two bodies emerge, the inevitable result of two spiritual baptisms.[21]

One body is conceived as consisting of ordinary believers. The other as Spirit-baptized super-saints. Pride tends to engender animosities and divisions. True unity in Christ is sacrificed to a false unity in an alleged deeper experience of the Holy Spirit. Christian brother is, accordingly, separated from Christian brother. The true oneness of God's people is thus imperilled.

Other believers have sought an experience of tongues or eradication of the old nature, and have fallen into many types of excess and fanaticism. That confusion of Spirit baptism with water baptism is the source of endless bitter controversy and denominational prejudice is well known to everybody.

2. *This misunderstanding obscures the gospel of grace.*

Someone will say that it matters very little so long as the promulgators of these misleading doctrines preach the gospel. The question is, however, how can anyone preach the gospel of the grace of God, while continually misrepresenting the teaching of the baptizing work of the Holy Spirit? What the gospel really is and what a multitude of uninstructed people are willing to call the gospel is quite a different thing.

L. S. Chafer's comment on this point is very pertinent:

> Where do the leaders of these great errors ever declare that God, impelled by infinite love and acting in sovereign grace, and on the ground of the absoluteness of the finished work of Christ, does save the chief of sinners eternally on no other condition than that he *believe?* Do they preach that being found in Christ every human merit and demerit, in the divine reckoning, passed; and the one who believes is so transferred

to the perfect merit of Christ that he will never perish, but will endure as Christ endures?

The preaching of the Gospel of Grace consists in the proclamation of these eternal glories, and apart from these announcements, *there is no gospel.*[22]

3. *Further, this misunderstanding perverts the truth of the believer's union with Christ.*

Oneness with Christ forms the only basis on which the believer can rest assured of any eternal standing before God. Little wonder teachers of these errors give no assurance of the security of the believer and of his unforfeitable position in Christ. Little wonder Christians, embracing these doctrines, doubt their salvation, or that they "have the Spirit," or that they are "sealed with the Spirit." Little wonder, then, Satan delights in these vagaries, since they deprive the believer of all security, rest, and joy in realization of union with Christ.

4. *Finally, this misunderstanding hinders a holy walk in the believer.*

It robs him of the chief incentive to such a walk, namely, an unobscured conception of his positions and possessions in Christ. "If ye then be risen with Christ, seek those things which are above" (Col 3:1). This is the true dynamic for a holy life. It is not surprising, therefore, to find the champions of these errors, while obscuring the genuine scriptural impulse to holiness, dragging in legalistic prohibitions and the bugbear of insecurity to frighten the believer into sanctity of life and to bolster up ebbing spirituality.

Who can ever estimate the vast amount of harm which has resulted from these misleading conceptions of truth? These errors threaten the very essence of the gospel message. Confusion in many quarters is appalling. The problem to state accurately the doctrine of the baptism of the Holy Spirit from the scriptural records, and to preach and teach it uncompromisingly, is one of the pressing needs of the hour.

3

The Baptism of the Spirit in the Gospels

IN THE MIDST of Israel's moral and spiritual decline and subsequent chastisements, the Holy Spirit through the prophets spoke of the coming Messiah. Hope was kept alive in the hearts of the godly remnant of the nation as the Spirit, through Isaiah, Jeremiah, Ezekiel, Joel, Zechariah, and Malachi, sang of the glories and splendors of Messiah's future reign. Then suddenly came an extended silence. For four long centuries, from the days of Malachi to those of John the Baptist, no God-inspired voice spoke the message of the kingdom of righteousness and peace.

At last the silence was broken by the powerful preaching of John at Jordan. His announcement was of the coming Messiah, whose distinguishing work would be to baptize with the Holy Spirit and with fire (Mt 3:11; Mk 1:8; Lk 3:16). In this climactic utterance John was like a scribe instructed in the kingdom of heaven, and bringing forth "out of his treasure things new and old" (Mt 13:52). The prophecy concerning Messiah's coming in His first advent was certainly not new, nor yet the idea of His coming in judgment to baptize "with fire" at His second advent (Is 61:2; Mal 3:1-6; 4:1). But what was new was the astonishing pronouncement that the coming One would baptize with the Holy Spirit.

THE BAPTISM OF THE SPIRIT IN THE TEACHING OF JOHN THE BAPTIST

1. *The baptism of the Spirit announced by John is not once in view in the Old Testament.*

39

The essential nature of this new work of God's Spirit and its unique place in the divine program are such as to forbid its occurring, or even being predicted there. As it is the operation which unites to the church, the body of Christ (1 Co 12:13), its distinct function is to make of Jew and Gentile a wholly new thing—to merge them into the same body (Eph 3:6), to fuse them into an entirely unique entity, where, because of common union with the risen Christ, all earthly distinctions of Jew and Gentile disappear. This *is* the mystery. This is the making of the "twain one new man" realized in the formation of the church (Eph 2:15). This is the miracle which the baptism with the Spirit accomplishes corporately, as it unites each believer to Christ individually.

The church is said to be a mystery (Eph 3:3), the mystery of Christ (Eph 3:4). It was foretold, but not explained by the Saviour (Mt 16:18). It was a truth unknown and unrevealed to anyone in Old Testament times (Eph 3:5), indeed a revelation and purpose "hid in God" throughout the ages (Eph 3:9), first realized historically at Pentecost, and first revealed doctrinally to the apostle Paul (Eph 3:3, 7).

In Romans 16:25 the apostle speaks of the church as the "revelation of the mystery," and says it "was kept secret since the world began" (Ro 16:25). He refers to the same mystery, the church, in Colossians 1:26 as that "which hath been hid from ages and from generations, but now is made manifest to his saints."

An examination of the Old Testament will confirm the testimony of the New. That the Gentiles were to be saved was no mystery. Moses, Isaiah, Hosea, and others told of Israel's blindness, and consequent mercy to the Gentiles (Deu 32:21; Is 42:6, 7; 65:1; Ho 1:10; 2:23). Joel sang of the outpouring of God's Spirit upon "all flesh" (Joel 2:28). Search will be made in vain, however, for the slightest reference to the church as the body of Christ, or to the Spirit's distinctive New Testament ministry of baptizing Jew and Gentile into one body.

It is true the Feast of Pentecost (Lev 23:15-22) typified the coming of the Holy Spirit to form the church on earth, but the meaning of the type was unrevealed to Old Testament saints.[1]

They were quite familiar with the two wave-loaves which were offered fifty days after the wave-sheaf, and were doubtless impressed with the fact that it was no longer a question of a sheaf of grain loosely bound together as in the Feast of First Fruits. But the significance of the union of the particles brought about by grinding the grain into flour and baking it with leaven into two loaves was hidden from them.

That this procedure symbolized the Holy Spirit's ministry at Pentecost (Ac 2:1-4) uniting the separate disciples into one organism (1 Co 10:16, 17; 12:12, 13, 20) was, of course, unknown to them. Nor did they realize that the two loaves represented two separate classes who were to form the one church, Jew (Ac 2) and Gentile (Ac 10), nor that the leaven pictured the truth that New Testament believers, although saved and constituted perfect positionally in Christ, experientially still were to possess a corrupt old nature that was to be kept in the place of death by the power of the Holy Spirit.

Other ministries of the Spirit (exclusive of the baptizing work) appear in the Old Testament, but not continually and perpetually, and in an abiding sense (as in this age), but only as occasion demanded. It is evident that Old Testament saints were regenerated, and, no doubt, Ridout is correct in calling regeneration "the common blessing of all dispensations."[2] The Spirit is said to have indwelt Joseph (Gen 41:38, 39), and Joshua (Num 27:18), but the indwelling apparently was not permanent or abiding (Ps 51:11), nor universal among Old Testament saints.[3]

The Spirit "came upon" Gideon (Judg 6:34), Amasai (1 Ch 12:18), Zechariah, the son of Jehoida (2 Ch 24:20), and literally clothed himself with these men to accomplish some specific work. It was not that these men were clothed with the Spirit, but rather the Spirit clothed himself with them. Likewise, the Spirit of the Lord came mightily upon Samson (Judg 14:6), Saul (1 Sa 10:10) and David (1 Sa 16:13). But "God the Holy Ghost is present, now, with the Church upon earth, in a much more special way than in the days of old."[4] What is noteworthy in the old dispensation "is the sovereign action and peculiar wisdom of the Holy Ghost in taking up certain vessels for His purpose."[5]

Thus appears the contrast between the work of the Holy Spirit in the Old Testament, and His present work of baptizing *every* believer into the body (1 Co 12:13), indwelling *every* believer forever (Jn 14:16) and sealing *every* believer eternally for glory (Eph 4:30), with the privilege of *every* believer, even the humblest, of being constantly filled with the Spirit. What kings, prophets, priests, and mighty men then enjoyed only temporarily can now be enjoyed by the lowliest perpetually. "Before Christ, the Spirit's work, as well as all God's ways, was one of *preparation;* after the descent of the Spirit at Pentecost, and in connection with the Church it was a time of *realization.*"[6] Owen likewise describes the work of the Holy Spirit under the Old Testament as "preparatory" to Christ "and the great work of the new creation in and by him."[7]

2. *The baptism of the Spirit announced by John is a unique operation confined to this present age from Pentecost to the rapture.*

Announced by John the Baptist as future to his time and ministry, and still future at the close of the forty-day, post-resurrection ministry of Jesus, our Saviour's statement definitely fixes the time of its occurrence as "not many days hence" (Ac 1:5). That it occurred between Acts 1:5 and 11:16 with regard to both Jew and Gentile, is obvious from Peter's words describing the event in Cornelius' house: "And as I began to speak, the Holy Ghost fell on them, as on us at the beginning. Then remembered I the word of the Lord, how that he said, John indeed baptized with water; but ye shall be baptized with the Holy Ghost" (Ac 11:15, 16).

It is clear, then, that the baptism of the Holy Spirit occurred on the day of Pentecost (Ac 2) and in the house of Cornelius (Ac 10). This is commonly recognized. But what is not recognized by many Christians (and what is responsible for appalling misunderstanding and widespread malpractice) is the important fact that the baptizing work of the Holy Spirit in Acts in inaugurating a new age has a dispensational significance, uniting believing Jew and Gentile to the body of Christ, of which our Lord is head.

To ignore this age-inaugurating aspect of the Spirit's work and to make His baptizing ministry at Pentecost and at Caesarea a second distinct work of grace or a so-called enduement with power is to becloud the sufficiency of the work of Christ and the believer's perfect position in Him, and to introduce irreconcilable contradiction between the Acts of the Apostles and the clear teaching of the epistles. There the inescapable truth is declared that the baptizing work of the Spirit is universal among Christians (1 Co 12:13) and the basis of all their blessings in Christ (Ro 6:3-5; Eph 1:3). To confound the baptism with the Spirit with a subsequent experience of power is to ignore the fact that this is a term "to cover the whole work of the Spirit from the beginning to the end of the believer's life. It is not some special distinct experience; but every distinct experience that may arise will be a fuller knowledge of all that is wrapped up and included in the Baptism in (with) the Spirit."[8]

The apostle's reference to baptism as one of the seven unities binding Christians together is confirmatory of the universal character of the baptizing work of the Spirit among Christians—"One Lord, one faith, one baptism" (Eph 4:5). Despite variety of interpretation to which this verse is commonly subjected, that the reference is manifestly to the baptizing work of the Spirit is indicated by the simple fact that it refers to spiritual realities which constitute the basis of the unity that characterizes all Christians. All have the same Lord, all have the same faith or essential body of truth, all are united organically into one body by one operation, the baptism of the Holy Spirit. Correctly René Pache calls this spiritual baptism of Ephesians 4:5 "la base spirituelle de l' Eglise" (the Church's spiritual basis[9]).

Not only is the believer brought into the body of Christ by the baptizing work of the Spirit, but into Christ Himself. This baptism into Christ is explained by the apostle Paul as an identification with the crucified and risen Saviour in the experiences of His death, burial, and resurrection.[10] "Know ye not, that so

many of us as were baptized into Jesus Christ were baptized
into his death? Therefore, we are buried with him by baptism
into death: that like as Christ was raised from the dead by the
glory of the Father, even so we also should walk in newness of
life" (Ro 6:3-4).

This same operation is called in 1 Corinthians 12:13 a baptism into the body of Christ. But since Christ is the Head of
the body (Eph 1:20-23), being baptized into Him is being
vitally united to His body, the church. On the day of Pentecost,
the Spirit began the formation of this new body for Christ and
will continue to add to it until it is completed.

The outcalling of the church is revealed in Scripture as the
distinctive dispensational ministry of the Holy Spirit in this
age.[11] At the first church council in Jerusalem, Simeon announced the program for this church age, pointing out how
God for the first time in the household of Cornelius (Acts 10)
"did visit the Gentiles to take out of them a people for his
name" (Ac 15:14).

Simeon also described the divine purpose for the era following the church age. "After this [the completion of the church]
I will return, and will build again the tabernacle of David,
which is fallen down" (Ac 15:16). This marks the time at
length come when the Lord "will restore again the kingdom to
Israel" (Ac 1:6), which kingdom the disciples erroneously
thought was to be set up at the time of Christ's ascension.

The Lord's building again the tabernacle of David at His
second advent signifies His divine purpose to reestablish the
Davidic rule over Israel in the millennial period (2 Sa 7:8-17;
Lk 1:31-33) that the remainder of Israel may seek after the
Lord (Zec 13:1, 2), as well as the Gentiles who will survive
the decimating judgments preceding the establishment of the
kingdom (Zec 8:21, 22).[12]

When the church is completed, and the last believer baptized
into the body of Christ, the redeemed of this age will be taken
out of the earth—the living changed, the dead raised, and both
caught up to meet the Lord in the air to be forever with the
Lord (1 Th 4:13-18; 1 Co 15:51-53).

Since the Holy Spirit came on the day of Pentecost and has

been resident upon the earth in the redeemed ever since (1 Co 6:19), the completion of the body of Christ and its removal from the earth will of necessity involve the removal of the Holy Spirit in the distinctive sense in which He came to form the body of Christ.

Is there any Scripture that would suggest the removal of the Holy Spirit in the special sense which marked His advent at Pentecost? Such a Scripture is 2 Thessalonians 2:7, 8: "For the mystery of lawlessness doth already work: only there is one that restraineth now, until he be taken out of the way. And then shall be revealed the lawless one" (American Revised Version).

Despite diversity of opinion as to the identity of the "one that restraineth," He is clearly the Holy Spirit in the light of 1 John 4:2, 3.[13] Two opposing spirits are set forth—the Spirit of God energizing the confession that Jesus Christ is come in the flesh, and the spirit of the Antichrist denying this great truth of the incarnation. This spirit will energize the lawless one, the Antichrist, who will arrogate to himself false Messianic claims, opposing and exalting himself "above all that is called God, or that is worshipped; so that he as God sitteth in the temple of God, shewing himself that he is God" (2 Th 2:4).

In the light of Scripture the restrainer of 2 Thessalonians 2:7 is the Holy Spirit.[14] He keeps Satan from producing his masterpiece, the man of sin, or Antichrist, of the tribulation period. A part of His important ministry in this age is to hold back the full development of sin and lawlessness until the church is complete. It is then that the Holy Spirit will be taken out of the way, which means the Holy Spirit will be removed from the earth scene as the restrainer of evil and the baptizer into the body of Christ.

As the restrainer of evil, the Holy Spirit resides in the church, the body of Christ, indwelling individual believers whose bodies are the temple of the Holy Spirit, and forming these corporately into a "holy temple in the Lord . . . for an habitation of God through the Spirit" (Eph 2:21-22). So indwelling the church and each individual member of it as a corporate unity, the Holy Spirit makes Christians "light in the Lord" (Eph 5:8) to dispel darkness in this present age, and salt (Mt 5:13) to counteract moral and spiritual degeneracy and putrefaction. Sin and apostasy will develop with fearful rapidity when the church of God is no longer in the world, culminating in world-wide lawlessness and the revelation of the lawless one of the end time (2 Th 2:3-12).

As the baptizer into the body of Christ, the Holy Spirit came on the day of Pentecost and has been performing this unique ministry throughout this age. But when God has completed His visitation to the Gentiles to take out of them the full number of people for His name (Ac 15:14), together with the full number of Israel comprising the "remnant according to the election of grace" (Ro 11:5), making "of twain one new man" (Eph 2:15), there will be no longer any need for the Spirit's baptizing work, and hence like His work of restraining evil in this present age, it will cease.[15]

However, there is a slight difference between the cessation of the restraining and baptizing work of the Spirit at the end of the church age. In the case of the Spirit's baptizing work, the cessation is complete, and this ministry is a unique feature of the church age from Pentecost to the rapture. It occurs in no other dispensation. It is always regarded as future until the day of Pentecost, and occurs only presently in reference to the church, the body of Christ (1 Co 12:13). It is never found after the outtaking of the church nor in the millennium.

In the case of the Spirit's ministry in restraining sin, this activity will certainly cease to a high degree, but will evidently not be total (cf. Rev 7:2f; 12:6, 14-16). The reason is simple. Although the Holy Spirit will be removed in the particular sense in which He came at Pentecost to be resident in the church, this does not mean that there will be no ministry of the Holy Spirit in the tribulation period any more than it means that there was no ministry of the Holy Spirit before Pentecost. He, the Spirit, the restrainer, will be removed from the world as resident here and reassume His position as omnipresent only.

A great multitude will be saved during the tribulation period (Rev 7:9-11). They will, of course, be saved by the Holy Spirit. But how can this be if the Holy Spirit is removed? He is removed, as the Scriptures indicate, as the baptizer into the body of Christ and, to a large extent, as the restrainer of evil. Evidently there will be a return to Old Testament and pre-Pentecost conditions.

Tribulation saints will be saved as Old Testament believers were saved, by the Holy Spirit coming to individuals and regenerating them. However it is not revealed that the tribulation saints, whether Gentile converts or the Jewish remnant, will be permanently indwelt and sealed by the Holy Spirit (as every believer now is), with the added privilege of being filled with the Spirit.

Whether or not the Spirit will permanently indwell and seal tribulation believers, there will be those, like the Jewish remnant, who will be filled with the Spirit, as Old Testament saints were filled, for the special task of proclaiming the worldwide message of the gospel of the kingdom (Mt 24:14).

The important thing to remember, however, is that the Spirit's ministry then will be purely individualistic. There will be no corporate ministry of baptizing believers into *one* body. That ministry is confined strictly to this age of grace and the outcalling of the church.

3. *The baptism of the Spirit announced by John was prophetic.*

In each of the four recorded references which the forerunner made to this divine baptism (Mt 3:11; Mk 1:8; Lk 3:16; Jn 1:32, 33), he spoke of it as something beyond himself, his message, and his age.[16] In each case, too, he spoke of Christ as the baptizer. In the light of this fact, it is amazing to note that the gospels, which chronicle the life and ministry of our Lord, have no account of this spiritual baptism, except the prophecy of it. The baptizer was to baptize no one until He should be put to death, rise again, and ascend back to heaven. As the baptizer with the Holy Spirit, He was the giver of the original ascension gift (Jn 16:7). He sent the Comforter to take His place.

When the Paraclete came at Pentecost to undertake all the ministries committed to Him in this age, our Lord, by virtue of His sending the Spirit, is said to be the baptizer with the

Spirit, since the formation of His mystical body by the divine baptism was the distinctive purpose to be accomplished in the new era which was inaugurated. However, after the Spirit took up residence upon the earth in the church and after He had undertaken His regular work of uniting both Jew and Gentile in the one body, He and not Christ is spoken of as the agent or baptizer (1 Co 12:13), as the normal course of the age is established.

In two of the four gospel references to Christ as the baptizer with the Holy Spirit, John the Baptist refers to our Lord as the baptizer "with fire" (Mt 3:11; Lk 3:16). Some expositors have attempted to find a fulfillment of this prophecy at Pentecost in the "cloven tongues like as of fire" (Ac 2:3).[17] Others have construed it as an amplification of the baptism of the Holy Spirit and an experience attainable in this present age, a so-called second Pentecost.[18] Both interpretations are erroneous.

It is clear from the immediate context of this reference to baptism with fire (Mt 3:9-12; Lk 3:16, 17) and from the general testimony of Scripture that it is connected with judgment and the second coming. As John F. Walvoord observes, "While the Church Age is introduced by the baptism of the Spirit, the kingdom age is to be introduced with a baptism of fire."[19]

When Christ comes the second time, the axe will be laid to the root of the trees, and "every tree which bringeth not forth good fruit" will be "hewn down, and cast into the fire" (Mt 3:10). His winnowing fan will be in His hand, "and he will throughly purge his floor, and gather his wheat into the garner; but he will burn up the chaff with unquenchable fire" (Mt 3:12).

The general testimony of Scripture likewise relates this baptism of fire with the second advent. Acts 1:5 is conclusive: Christ said to His disciples, "John truly baptized with water, but ye shall be baptized with the Holy Ghost not many days hence." Our Lord is quoting what John said previously, yet He does not mention baptism with fire. A. C. Gaebelein aptly remarks that if our Lord "had added, *and with fire*, it would clearly prove that the baptism connected with His first coming is a baptism with the Holy Spirit *and* fire. But he leaves out the fire because it stands in connection with His second coming. Thus it is seen in the entire prophetic Word, which speaks of the day of wrath and vengeance as being a day of burning and fire."[20]

At first, it might appear singular that John the Baptist should speak of both advents in such intimate connection, but it must be remembered he still belonged to the old economy and expressed himself as many of the Old Testament prophets did, who frequently spoke in one clause of both the Lord's first and second appearing.

The baptism with fire, accordingly, has no connection with Spirit baptism. To interpret wrongly these Scriptures as supporting such a connection is unsound and can produce much confusion in matters of both faith and practice. It is unscriptural to pray for a baptism with fire, for there is no such baptism now. In fact, no believer can pray for the flaming fire to fall upon him, for the simple reason he has been delivered from that wrath by the blood of Christ.

THE BAPTISM OF THE SPIRIT IN THE TEACHING OF CHRIST

1. *The baptism of the Spirit was effected by Christ but was not effective upon Christ.*

It is quite obvious that the four recorded references in the gospels to the baptizing work of the Spirit connect this ministry with our Lord as the baptizer. This is done, as noted, because this operation of the Spirit springs from the death, burial, resurrection, and ascension of the Redeemer and His consequent sending of the Holy Spirit as His ascension gift, to perform among other activities, His baptizing work.

However, a common mistake is to identify the baptizer *with* the Holy Spirit as also the one baptized *by* the Holy Spirit.[21] Some Bible teachers assert that Jesus was baptized with the Holy Spirit at His baptism by John in the Jordan. Torrey says that Jesus never entered His public ministry "until He was baptized with the Holy Spirit."[22]

That our Lord was anointed by the Holy Spirit and divinely filled without measure (cf. Jn 3:34) is certain. But to confuse this anointing with the baptizing work of the Spirit displays serious misunderstanding of the essential nature of Spirit baptism.

Our Lord could not possibly have been baptized by the Spirit for the following reasons. All the references to this operation are prophetic in the gospels, the event not becoming historical until Pentecost, after the earthly ministry of our Lord was completed. Because the baptism of the Spirit was a *result* of Christ's finished work of redemption, it was impossible that it should occur *before* His death, resurrection, and ascension. It was also impossible that it should not take place *after* these events.

Moreover, there is not the slightest reason that our Lord should have been baptized by the Spirit. From a consideration of the purpose of that baptism, it was impossible that He should be so baptized.[23] As the Son of God, He possessed in addition to a divine nature, a sinless human nature that needed to be anointed and filled with the Holy Spirit, as it was at Jordan. But as Son of God and Son of man, He was already one with the Father (Jn 10:30), and needed no spiritual baptism to make Him one.

It was on the basis of His oneness with the Father and in view of His approaching redemptive work on the cross and the subsequent giving of the Holy Spirit to perform His baptizing work that our Lord prayed for the oneness not only of His immediate circle of disciples, but "for them also who *shall believe*" on Him "through their word that they all may be one, as thou, Father, art in me, and I in thee, that they also may be one in us" (Jn 17:20, 21).

Considering both His person and work, our Lord could not possibly have been baptized with the Spirit. His person needed no such baptism. He was one with the Father. His work rendered such a spiritual operation upon Himself impossible. His ministry leading to His redemptive work on the cross was at

the time of his appearance before John at Jordan only beginning. The Spirit's baptizing work, on the other hand, is based
upon a *finished* work and concerns uniting believers to the risen,
ascended Christ, thus making them one with the Son as the Son
is one with the Father. Accordingly, under no consideration
can the baptizer with the Holy Spirit be said to be the one baptized with the Holy Spirit.

What, then, did occur when Jesus was baptized by John in
Jordan (Mt 3:13-15) and the "Holy Spirit descended in a
bodily shape like a dove upon him" (Lk 3:21, 22)? In the
light of our Saviour's own explanation of the event as a fulfilling of "all righteousness" (Mt 3:15), and in the light of the
priesthood as it appertained to our Lord's redemptive ministry,
the event clearly marked "His formal induction into the office
of Priest."[24]

At His baptism Christ received His anointing with the Holy
Spirit (Mt 3:16) for His threefold office of prophet, priest, and
king, which is comprehensively descriptive of His entire ministry. Yet the essence of His redemptive work does not lie in
His prophetic or kingly office, but in His consecration as a
priest, the Great High Priest, for it was in this office He offered not "the blood of bulls and goats," but Himself in order
to put away sin (Heb 9:24-26). It is this consecration to His
priesthood that comes into clearest view in the baptismal scene.

In His reference to fulfilling all righteousness lies the import
and motive of His baptism. Jesus meant the righteousness of
the Mosaic law, which was in force till His death on Calvary,
and to which he carefully conformed. The Levitical law required that all priests be consecrated when they "began to be
about thirty years of age," as was the case with Jesus (Lk 3:23;
cf. Num 4:3). The consecration was twofold—first the washing, then the anointing (Ex 29:4-7; Lev 8:6-36). Aaron
shared in the washing, being a sinner and needing it, and furnishing the type of the baptism of Christ, Who, not being a
sinner Himself and not needing it, nevertheless identified Himself with sinners, and fulfilled the Aaronic type.

After the washing came the anointing (Ex 29:5-7). When

John the Baptist at Jordan's bank "washed" (baptized) Jesus, the heavens were opened and the Holy Spirit came upon Him. This was the priestly anointing of Him who was not only a priest by divine appointment, but an eternal priest (Ps 110:4) and who was thus divinely consecrated for the work of redemption (Mt 3:16; Ac 4:27; 10:38).

Upon the foundation of the finished work of redemption our Lord gave the Holy Spirit to regenerate, indwell, seal, and baptize each believer into organic union with Himself and with each other in Him. In this role He was the baptizer with the Holy Spirit.

2. *The baptism of the Spirit bears vital relationship to Christ's teaching and was included in the upper room discourse.*

Our Lord while on earth taught that the Father in answer to prayer would "give the Holy Spirit to them that ask Him" (Lk 11:13). This promise, of course, was pre-Pentecost and was spoken under the old economy, when the Spirit of God came upon men and departed according to divine sovereign will. For a man to ask for, much less receive, the Spirit was a staggering, new concept to a Jew. It was in advance of the fulfillment of Joel 2:28, 29, and there is no evidence that any asked for the Spirit, claiming this promise.[25]

To apply this teaching to the present age is an error. It assumes that the ministry of the Holy Spirit is the same in every dispensation and forgets Pentecost, ignoring the fact that every believer now has the indwelling Spirit.[26] It was the ascended Christ who asked the Father for the Spirit as the ascension gift (Jn 14:16), and no believer now—baptized and indwelt with the Spirit as he is—need ever ask for Him. He possesses the Holy Spirit, not because he has prayed or asked for Him, but because he has Him as a free gift by virtue of simple faith in the crucified and risen Saviour.

In John 7:37-39 Jesus gives important instruction concerning the Spirit. John describes the Spirit's circumscribed activity in the old economy in these words: "The Holy Spirit was not yet (given)," with the appended reason, "because Jesus was not yet glorified" (Jn 7:39). This amazing statement does not mean that the Holy Spirit was not present nor did not have a vital ministry in Old Testament times and in pre-Pentecost experience. It does mean, however, that as a result of the death, burial, resurrection, ascension of our Lord, and His exaltation at the Father's right hand, the Holy Spirit would be given in such an abundant manner that the contrast between the old dispensation of limited spiritual blessing and the new age of the Holy Spirit ushered in at Pentecost could be described in these terms: "The Holy Spirit was not yet—the Holy Spirit *now is.*"

As Lewis Sperry Chafer points out: "Incidentally a very clear distinction is drawn here between the saints of the former dispensation and those of the present. New and far-reaching realities certainly belong to those who are identified with the glorified Christ."[27] Tenney says, "The implication is clear that only after the death of Christ could the Spirit begin the fullest work."[28]

What are the "new and far-reaching realities" our Saviour prophetically mentions in this passage, "which belong to those who are identified with the glorified Christ"? The most embracing is that *all* who believe on Christ as Saviour shall receive the Holy Spirit as an automatic accompaniment to their salvation (cf. Gal 3:2). And not only so, but upon the same basis of faith in Christ as Lord may receive the Spirit in His fullness. "If any man is thirsty, let him come to Me and drink. He who believes in Me, as the Scripture said, From his innermost being shall flow rivers of living water" (Jn 7:37, 38, NASB).

Our Lord's words clearly predict the Spirit's coming at Pentecost to perform individually and corporately during this age His various ministries of regenerating, baptizing, indwelling, sealing, and filling. His prophecy pictures the coming of the Spirit as a plentiful and beneficent outpouring hitherto unknown and unexperienced. Yet no other ministry so well illustrates the contrast between the old dispensation and the new as the Spirit's baptizing work. All the other ministries were present, at least upon occasion, in the pre-Pentecost era. But not the baptizing work of the Spirit. This is a feature of the church age which is unique and illustrates the statement, "The Holy Spirit was not yet given."

Moreover, the prediction does not view the effect of the Spirit's ministry upon the believer himself so much as the result upon his testimony and ministry to others. The implication is, of course, that the believer himself will be refreshed by drinking, but the emphasis is upon the believer's augmented ability to refresh others. The expression *rivers of living water* portrays the unparalleled spiritual blessings of the present age, elsewhere pictured under the figure of a "well of water springing up into everlasting life" (Jn 4:14), and give the idea of fullest refreshment. The baptism of the Spirit Jesus would bring would place the believer in a new sphere where such blessing would be possible.

As Leon Morris states,

> Jesus came that men might be brought into contact with the divine Spirit. But baptism is a figure which stresses abundant supply. So John will mean that the Spirit leads men into the infinite divine spiritual resources. This had not been possible previously, for there is a quality of life that Christ and none other makes available to men. Baptism with water had essentially a negative significance. It is a cleansing from—. But baptism with the Spirit is positive. It is the bestowal of new life in God.[29]

In the upper room discourse (Jn 14-16) Jesus promised that He Himself would pray the Father, and in answer to His prayer, the Comforter would come to abide permanently (Jn 14:15), and that now dwelling *with* them, He would then dwell *in* them (Jn 14:17). The prophecy of the permanent indwelling of the Spirit is thus a feature of Christ's parting instruction to His disciples before His death. It was also a further illustration of the circumscribed spiritual blessing of the prechurch age and the promise of greatly augmented spiritual privileges offered by the Spirit's advent.[30]

Likewise, our Lord alludes to the baptizing work of the Spirit in the new age. "In that day you shall know that I am in My Father, and *you in Me*, and I in you" (Jn 14:20, NASB).

"I in you" describes the Spirit's permanent indwelling in this age. "Ye in Me" indicates the baptizing ministry of the Spirit, for the only way a believer can be placed "in Christ" is by a spiritual baptism (Ro 6:3, 4; Col 1:12, 13; Gal 3:27).

In the Great Commission as recorded by Mark (16:15, 16) Jesus assuredly makes reference to the baptizing work of the Spirit. G. Campbell Morgan correctly observes: *"He that believeth* [that is the human condition] *and is baptized* [that is the divine miracle] *shall be saved.* When the negative side is stated, baptism is omitted, as being unnecessary; for he that disbelieveth cannot be baptized. If it is water baptism he can; but if it is the baptism of the Spirit, he cannot."[31]

In this much misunderstood passage, baptism is related to salvation as a vital and inseparable feature of it. To apply this to the ritual and not to real baptism brings this passage into collision with a multitude of other passages which set forth the gospel of grace as involving faith alone. Such an interpretation, at variance with the general tenor of Scripture, must be rejected.

The new relation of being in Christ is accomplished by the baptizing ministry of the Spirit and in this age of grace cannot possibly be absent in any case of genuine salvation. In contrast, it is quite possible for one to be unsaved and yet to have received ritual baptism. It also is true that all who are saved have been saved quite apart from ritual baptism.

Mark 16:16 contains a usage of speech quite common in Scripture: the main thought of a passage is amplified by one of the features in it. Luke 1:20 offers an illustration. "Thou shalt be dumb, and not able to speak." The concept of *dumb* is elaborated by the words *not able to speak.* Likewise in the text at hand, the word *believeth* is amplified by *and is baptized,* and with reference to Spirit baptism, which is an integral part of salvation.

3. *The baptism of the Spirit is the answer to Christ's prayer for Christian unity.*

In His great intercessory prayer in John 17, our Lord made many petitions. He prays that His joy may be fulfilled in His disciples (v. 13), that they might be kept from the evil (v. 15), that they might be sanctified (v. 17), and that they might be with Him to behold His glory (v. 24).

But the most amazing petition in this sublime chapter is the Saviour's intercession for Christian unity. By striking emphasis this feature stands out in bold relief. It is repeated over and over again in our Lord's requests. Notice verse 11: "Holy Father, keep through thine own name those whom thou hast given me, that they *may be one,* as we are." Verses 20, 21: "Neither pray I for these alone but for them also who shall believe on me through their word that they *all may be one, even as we are one.*" Verse 23: "I in them and thou in me, that they may be made perfect in one."

Has this petition of our Saviour been answered? Are Christians one in spite of the glaring evidences of disunity—interminable strife, sectarian divisions, doctrinal schisms, petty jealousies, and factional antagonisms reaching back into the centuries? The answer, of course, is our Saviour's prayer *was* answered. Could any prayer of His be unanswered? Christians are *one.* They are *all* one. Christian unity is a reality because the Holy Spirit has been outpoured.

Our Lord's supplication was answered in the coming of the Holy Spirit at Pentecost to perform His baptizing work then and throughout this age. At that time Jewish believers were baptized by the Spirit into organic union with Christ (Ac 2:47; 5:14). In the progressive dispensational outreach of the gospel the racially mongrel Samaritans were subsequently baptized into Christ (Ac 8). Gentile believers in Cornelius' house came under the same dispensational blessing (Ac 10).

Now, in the normal course of the age, all believers are so united to Christ the moment they believe on Christ as Saviour. "For by one Spirit are we *all* baptized into one body" (1 Co 12:13). "Know ye not, that so many of us as were baptized into Jesus Christ were baptized into His death? Therefore we are buried with him by baptism into death" (Ro 6:3, 4). "For as many of you as have been baptized into Christ have put on Christ" (Gal 3:27). "One body . . . one baptism, one God" (Eph 4:4-6). "For we are all members of his body, of his flesh and of his bones" (Eph 5:30). "Now ye are the body of Christ and members in particular" (1 Co 12:27). Christ "the head over all things to the church, which is his body" (Eph 1:22, 23).

The New Testament teaches that by the baptizing work of the Holy Spirit *all* believers, the youngest as well as the oldest, the weakest as well as the strongest, are so intimately joined to Christ that the union is as close and inseparable—as far as spiritual life is concerned—as the connection between the human head and the physical body.

Being joined to Christ, Christians are thereby joined to one another. But more wonderful still they are *all* one in Christ as the Father and the Son are one. And being joined to Christ, they are, in the words of the poet:

> Near to the heart of God
> Nearer I could not be,
> For in the person of His Son
> I am as near as He.
>
> AUTHOR UNKNOWN

This is the answer to Jesus' petition, "Holy Father, keep through thine own name those whom thou has given me, that they may be one, as we are" (Jn 17:11). "That they *all* may be one, as thou, Father, art in me and I in thee, that they also may be one in us" (v. 21). In the church of God (Ac 20:28) our Lord has thus united humanity to deity forever.

But the question of the obvious disunity among God's people presses for explanation. If all Christians are one in answer to our Lord's intercession, why are they so divided?

What is true of other aspects of spiritual truth must be again emphasized. The *factual,* insofar as the provision of God in the finished work of Christ is concerned, must be made *actual,* insofar as our experiential enjoyment of it is to be realized. This is to be accomplished by a worthy Christian walk (Eph 4:1-3) in the light of a correct understanding of the biblical basis of Christian unity (Eph 4:4-6).

It must be said, however, that no matter how Christians have bungled in the experiential realization of Christian unity, the fact remains that *all* Christians are one by the baptizing work of the Spirit in answer to our Lord's high priestly prayer in John 17. The reality of Christian unity must be made an actuality by our understanding of the biblical teaching and faith to put it into practice.

> From this prayer the conclusion must be drawn that an entirely new divine undertaking has been introduced into the world, its object being the outcalling of a company of saints each one of which company will have been perfected forever, being in Christ, and that each has attained to that exalted position by the one act of believing on Christ. So far as previous human relations to God are concerned, this is wholly new—even for the disciples themselves.[32]

With the historical occurrences of the baptism with the Holy Spirit in the Acts of the Apostles in answer to our Lord's prayer for Christian oneness, this wholly new human relationship to God becomes a reality in the formation of the church, the body of Christ.

4

The Baptism of the Spirit at Pentecost and at Samaria

THE DIVINE REVELATION concerning the Holy Spirit is progressive. Foregleams of His Person and work appear in the Old Testament. There He came upon whom He chose without any apparent reference to the spiritual condition of the person. Then John the Baptist arrived on the scene with a sweeping prophetic announcement concerning a new ministry, the baptism with the Holy Spirit, which would be inaugurated by the Messiah.

Christ Himself, during His earthly life, told His disciples that they might receive the Holy Spirit by asking the Father (Lk 11:13). He was no doubt preparing them for a more glorious unfolding of truth—that He would pray for the Comforter, who would come to remain permanently in each and every one of them *without* any asking whatever on their part (Jn 14:16-17).

On the evening of the day of His resurrection, a further step was taken. Jesus breathed on the disciples (Jn 20:22) and apparently gave them the Holy Spirit, possibly to equip them to receive the teaching of the forty days, and possibly because they themselves had failed to ask for the Spirit, according to the promise of Luke 11:13.

In the book of Acts the progressive revelation concerning the Spirit is unfolded more and more. What was prophetic in the gospels, with John the Baptist and Jesus, became historic in the apostles and early Christians. What was predicted and promised became realized and appropriated. Prophecy was translated into history, promise into experience. Pivotal and important is the development in the second chapter of Acts.

PENTECOST AND THE BAPTISM OF THE SPIRIT

W. H. Griffith Thomas notes as one of the important features of the book of Acts "the prominence given to the day of Pentecost."[1] This prominence is to be expected because of the age-inaugurating significance of the event. But second-blessing movements of the eighteenth century and particularly the Pentecostal and neo-Pentecostal trends of the twentieth century have given Acts 2 even greater emphasis. In the light of current church history it is safe to say that no portion of Scripture is so widely featured today or subject to more erroneous interpretation than the event of Pentecost. It is, therefore, necessary to inquire very carefully, "What does this [event] mean?" (Ac 2:12, NASB).

1. *Pentecost signifies the coming, the arrival and the taking up of permanent residence of the Holy Spirit in the new people of God on earth.*

The Holy Spirit, of course, is omnipresent. But so definitely was the new age to be characterized by the Spirit's intimate presence that our Lord, the greatest commentator on the meaning of Pentecost, declared that the Father would send the Spirit to take up His residence on the earth. His words in the upper room discourse looked forward to Pentecost. "And I will pray the Father, and he shall give you another Comforter that he may abide with you for ever" (Jn 14:16). The word *abide* (Greek *menei*) means "remain," and the thought is the Holy Spirit would come, arrive, and take up permanent residence on earth in the people of God "throughout the age."

Again with fulfillment at Pentecost in view, our Lord in the same discourse declared, "Nevertheless I tell you the truth; it is expedient for you that I go away, for if I go not away, the Comforter *will not come* to you; but if I depart, I will send him unto you. And when *he is come* [has arrived], he will reprove the world of sin, and of righteousness, and of judgment" (Jn 16:

7-8). "When he, the Spirit of truth, is come," our Lord continues, "he will guide you into all truth" (Jn 16:13).

Very clearly our Lord in these parting words to His disciples just before His death previewed the basic meaning of Pentecost. The Holy Spirit would arrive and take up permanent residence in believers for the duration of the age. In Acts 2 this is exactly what happened. The Holy Spirit arrived at Pentecost over nineteen hundred years ago. He has been indwelling the people of God corporately and each believer individually ever since (Ro 8:9; 1 Co 6:9), and has promised never to leave a child of God, whose body He indwells as a holy temple (Jn 14:16-18).

How unscriptural, then, to tarry or wait for the Holy Spirit to come, when he came long ago, and has been resident in the people of God ever since.

2. *Pentecost marks the giving, receiving, and depositing of the gift of the Spirit in the new people of God on earth.*

Our Lord promised this gift to His disciples as a going-away present. He was about to leave them. He told them of a gift by which they would be able to remember Him in a most wonderful way. "And I will pray the Father, and he shall give you another Comforter . . . even the Spirit of truth, whom the world cannot receive" (Jn 14:16-17). "If I depart, I will send him unto you" (Jn 16:7). "But the Comforter, which is the Holy Ghost, whom the Father will *send* in my name, he shall teach you" (Jn 14:26).

Our Lord's prediction of what would happen at Pentecost occurred exactly as foretold: the gift of the Holy Spirit was given, received, and permanently deposited. Moreover, the gift, the Holy Spirit Himself, was lavishly bestowed and His blessings copiously poured out.

How ridiculous to ask for the gift now, as if it had never been given, or attempt to receive it when it has been a permanent deposit of the people of God for many centuries, and its contents and benefits made available to every believer since the day of Pentecost. The moment a sinner believes on Christ, he enters into *all* the blessings of the gift of the Spirit by virtue of the great salvation he receives as a result of the permanently deposited gift of the Spirit in the church.

On the basis of the newly received gift at Pentecost and its permanent deposition in the church, Peter urged unsaved Jews to repent of their sin, and to share in the wealth of the outpoured gift of the Spirit. "Then Peter said unto them, Repent, and be baptized every one of you in the name of Jesus Christ for the remission of sins, and ye shall *receive the gift of the Holy Ghost.* For the promise is unto you, and to your children, and to all that are afar off, even as many as the Lord our God shall call" (Ac 2:38-39).

In this clear gospel call, the apostle was *not* offering something in addition to salvation, but the common salvation of the new era itself. The gift of the Spirit not only inaugurated the new age but introduced and mediated the great salvation, based upon the death and resurrection of Christ, now made available in the new age. The duly received and permanently deposited gift insured salvation throughout the age to all who would believe, as the apostle Peter declared.[2]

3. *Pentecost represents an unrepeated and unrepeatable event.*

It is as unrepeatable as the creation of the universe, the creation of man, the incarnation of Christ, His sinless life, vicarious death, glorious resurrection, or any other event of history. This fact becomes evident when it is realized the Holy Spirit could come, arrive, and take up permanent residence *only once,* which He did at Pentecost. Moreover, He could be given, received, and permanently deposited as God's free gift *only once,* which likewise occurred at Pentecost.

Moreover, the event of Pentecost took place at a specifically designated time (Ac 2:1), in fulfillment of a special Old Testament type (Lev 23:15-22), in a specially designated place, Jerusalem (Lk 24:49), upon a specially designated group (Ac 1:14), for a specific purpose (1 Co 12:12-26). Most important, it was designed to introduce a new order, *not* to be the recurring feature of the new order, once it was introduced.

Pentecost may be compared to the inauguration day of an

American president. The wind, the fire, and the tongues were like the inaugural parade, the inaugural oath, the inaugural balls. No one expects the events of the inaugural day to be repeated throughout the four-year term. Pentecost initiated a new epoch in the economy of God. No believer should rationally expect the introductory features to characterize the age or be repeated during the course of the age.

4. *Pentecost presents the advent of the Spirit and the reception of the gift of the Spirit to perform all his ministries in this age.*

The event marks the advent of the person of the Spirit, and the gift is the person. *All* the ministries of the Person of the Spirit are included in the gift. L. S. Chafer lists some thirty-five of these operations which the Spirit performs in the believer the moment he is saved.[3] The Spirit performed these ministries upon all believers at Pentecost when He arrived to take up permanent residence in the people of God. As resident in the church He has been performing these ministries ever since in those who believe in Christ and are saved. Moreover, He performs *all* these ministries at the moment of salvation and as vital and inseparable constituents of salvation, never as something in addition to salvation.

The gift—given, received, and permanently deposited in God's people at Pentecost—contains all the ministries. The permanent deposit of the gift assures instant salvation to the sinner the moment he believes. His salvation is *not* a receiving of the Spirit as at Pentecost, but an automatic entrance into all the benefits of the permanently deposited gift of the Spirit. This gift has been available to each believing sinner the moment he believes, ever since its bestowal at Pentecost.

Of the thirty-five or so ministries the Holy Spirit accomplishes in the believing sinner at the moment of salvation, five are crucial and illustrative of the rest. These are the regenerating, baptizing, indwelling, and sealing ministries, together with the privilege of the filling ministry. All these transactions of the Spirit are performed in the believer the moment he is saved, constituting his "so great salvation" (Heb 2:3). They are received solely on the basis of faith as ministries of the deposited "free gift" of the Spirit and form the constituent elements of the *free gift* of salvation assured those who believe the gospel of grace.

The ministry of regeneration. Old Testament saints were regenerated by faith, as were Abraham and David (Ro 4:1-25) and the disciples of Jesus before Pentecost (Lk 10:20). This does not mean, however, that what happened to Jesus' disciples at Pentecost was something in addition to salvation, a sort of second work of grace. *They received the common salvation of the new era,* purchased by Christ on the cross, attested by Christ's glorious resurrection, and mediated by the outpoured gift of the Spirit consequent upon Christ's ascension to heaven.

The experience of Jesus' disciples at Pentecost cannot be used as a norm for today, a simple fact so universally overlooked in our time by Pentecostal and neo-Pentecostal believers and by Christians in general who subscribe to what may be called second-blessing theology.[4] It must never be forgotten that Old Testament saints who passed through the events recorded in the second chapter of Acts were passing from one age to another. Pentecost marked the inauguration of the new era in which the "so great salvation" (Heb 2:3) provided by Christ on the cross was to be wrought in believers by the Spirit. Our Lord shortly before His death foretold this truth to His disciples in the Upper Room (Jn 14:16-20; 16:12-13). Now, that which had not yet become an actuality, was to become an accomplished transaction in the position and experience of the disciples.

All of this means, if our Lord's words are to be taken seriously, that both the *content* and *character* of pre-cross salvation were not the same as the *content* and *character* of post-cross salvation mediated for the first time to fallen humanity at Pentecost. This does not mean that God has more than one way of salvation or more than one kind of salvation. Salvation in every age is solely by grace through faith. It is always grounded in the finished redemption of Christ, whether looking forward to it in its pre-cross aspect or back to it in its post-cross phase.

As to content, pre-cross salvation embraced regeneration

(Gen 15:6; Jn 3:10), but *not* certain other ministries of the Spirit, as Jesus indicated in His upper room discourse (Jn 14-16), as He previewed what would happen when the Spirit would come at Pentecost (see Jn 14:17-20). If the so-great-salvation Jesus foretold would become available as the result of His death, burial, resurrection, ascension and bestowal of the Spirit, not only would certain ministries be added, but all the operations of the Spirit in a now-accomplished salvation would be evidenced in a deeper, more permanent form.

How precarious then for present-day charismatic Christianity to insist that because pre-Pentecostal saints were born again, therefore, what happened to them at Pentecost was something in addition to salvation. Actually these believers were receiving the common salvation of the new age which was being opened to them as well as to all who would believe the gospel of the free gift of salvation based upon a crucified and risen Saviour.

Now that the new era has been established and the normal course of the age attained for Jew (Ac 2), racially mongrel Samaritan (Ac 8), and pure Gentile (Ac 10), it is impossible for anyone to be born again (saved) and not receive the great salvation of the new age. This situation by contrast was not possible nor actual for Jesus' disciples. They were in the unique situation of being transported from the Old to the New Testament era. This fact of the great event of Pentecost must be firmly borne in mind if what took place then is to be correctly comprehended.

The ministry of baptism. It was the Spirit's baptizing ministry that was unique to Pentecost and occurred for the first time as the Spirit came from heaven and arrived on earth, and the gift of the Spirit was given and received. That this ministry of the Spirit was never operative in the Old Testament and was still future during the ministry of John the Baptist and Jesus is easily seen from John's predictions of it in the gospels (Mt 3:11; Mk 1:8; Lk 3:16-17; Jn 1:33) and the fact that at the ascension of our Lord ten days before Pentecost, it was still a future event (Ac 1:5).

That the Spirit performed His unique baptizing operation *at*

Pentecost is backed up by Peter's explanation of that event at Cornelius' home in Caesarea (Ac 10:44-48). "And as I began to speak, the Holy Ghost fell on them, as on us at the beginning. Then remembered I the word of the Lord, how that he said, John indeed baptized with water; but ye shall be baptized with the Holy Ghost" (Ac 11:15-16).

The Gentile Cornelius, who doubtless was regenerated before Peter came to Caesarea (Ac 10:2-4), apparently did not receive the common salvation ministered by the outpoured gift of the Spirit upon the Gentiles. This is clearly declared by the angel who had appeared to Cornelius and said that Peter would tell him "words" by which he and all his household should "be saved" (Ac 11:14).

The baptizing work of the Holy Spirit, effective upon Jews at Pentecost and Gentiles in the home of Cornelius, did *not* bring them a second blessing subsequent to their salvation, but marked their initiation into the common salvation of the new age itself. The disciples of Jesus before Pentecost were in a spiritual condition not essentially different from that of Cornelius before Peter brought him the gospel of a crucified and risen Lord. Both received the great salvation Christ offered those who would believe on Him.

Pentecostals and neo-Pentecostals may certainly relate the event of Pentecost to the baptism of the Spirit, for it is so related in the context of Scripture (Ac 1:5; 11:14-16). Yet there is no authority for connecting the ten-day period of waiting with this divine baptism. The disciples were not "tarrying" for the baptism of the Spirit, but waiting for the coming of the Spirit. When the Comforter arrived, He united those who previously had been only followers of the Messiah, into members vitally united to the risen Lord and to one another in His mystical body (1 Co 12:13). No longer were they to be a company of separate units, a mere loose association of individuals, having only a broad bond of sympathy in their common love for Christ. Miraculously and instantaneously they were fused into a corporate unity, the church of Jesus Christ, "which made them one with Him and with each other."[5]

The advent of the Spirit to perform His ministry of baptizing affected the relation of the whole human race to God. It brought about a new creation, consisting of Christ, the new Adam, and all those united to Him. It introduced into the world a new temple, the church. "Ye are the temple of God" (1 Co 3:16). Individually each believer became a temple. Collectively believers became a "habitation of God through the Spirit" (Eph 2:22).

The one hundred and twenty in the upper room were no longer a mere company, but Christ's church. They became a temple of praise, prayer, and prophecy. They were converted into a divine institution of which the old temple with its offerings, ritual, and priesthood was prophetic. The temple was destined to expand and grow. As men enter it through Christ, the door of the church, the Spirit baptizes them into living union with Him.

Pentecost was the bestowal of the Holy Spirit as the gift of God. The baptism was an inseparable part of that gift. Man had no claim upon God for that great bestowal. Pentecostal and neo-Pentecostal views that attach various conditions for the Spirit's baptism miss the free nature of the gift and fall into a variation of Galatian legalism.[6] In answer to the Pentecostal conditions the reply may be, "the faith which is so assiduously cultivated God grants; the Holy Spirit who is so scrupulously sought God gives—and the means is simply the divine gospel which is the power of *God* unto salvation (cf. Ro 1:16)."[7]

It is clear, therefore, that the baptism of the Spirit is never to be tarried for, prayed for, or sought for. As a vital part of God's free gift of salvation, it is the heritage of every child of God. It is guaranteed him the moment he believes because of the presence of the risen Christ in heaven.[8]

The ministry of indwelling. Pentecost also marked the coming of the Spirit to accomplish His ministry of indwelling. Although Old Testament saints such as Joseph (Gen 41:38-39) and Joshua (Num 27:18) were indwelt by the Spirit, this ministry appears not to have been universal or permanent (cf. Judg 16:20; 1 Sa 16:14; Ps 51:11). But at Pentecost the Spirit came not only to indwell each believer but to indwell him permanently. The Spirit also came to indwell the church corporately for the duration of the church age (Jn 14:16).

Our Lord foretold this truth to His disciples. He declared the Spirit was then *with* them and would soon be *in* them (Jn 14:17). After the Spirit's coming at Pentecost the Spirit was in them. He indwells every believer individually throughout the church age (Ro 8:9; 1 Co 6:19-20) and the church corporately (Eph 2:22).

The ministry of sealing. Pentecost also marked the coming of the Spirit to work out His ministry of sealing. Since the Holy Spirit came at Pentecost to indwell each believer, and since He Himself as the indwelling one is the seal (Eph 1:13; 4:30; 2 Co 1:22), it follows that all the one hundred and twenty and those saved at Pentecost, were stamped as God's own.

The ministry of filling. Pentecost also marked the coming of the Spirit to indwell and baptize the believer into vital union with Christ, thus endowing him with a position before God of spiritual fullness. Being placed "in Christ," God viewed the believers at Pentecost as "blessed with all spiritual blessings" (Eph 1:3). In this sphere of exalted standing and privilege, the believer has the opportunity and incentive to translate his position of fullness into an experience of that fullness in everyday living.

This means that God's great salvation dispensed at Pentecost brought with it spiritual completeness. God did not give His Spirit partially but completely. He did not grant a piecemeal salvation but a perfect one. This salvation was totally received at Pentecost. The positional fullness it brought to every believer became the basis for the experiential fullness, the actual filling of the Spirit (Ac 2:4) which was enjoyed on that occasion.

But the all-important fact is that the Pentecostal filling was part of the free gift. It was emphatically not something separated from or in addition to it. It was both the experience and the expression of salvation and what was divinely intended to be the normal operation of the indwelling Spirit.

Therefore, being part of the free gift, both positional fullness and experiential fullness are on the basis of simple faith.

However, this must be faith in what the believer is *in union with Christ,* not what he is in himself. It is trusting what Christ has done for him, not what he may do for Christ to obtain some spiritual experience.

Faith in what Christ has done for the believing sinner brings positional spiritual fullness (salvation). Faith in what the believer is in Christ brings experiential fullness (the infilling). But what must always be held in mind is that the baptism of the Spirit imparting positional fullness is not experiential fullness. The baptism is the ground of the infilling but not the experience of the filling, just as the foundation of a building is not the building itself.

The 120 disciples at Pentecost consequently received the Spirit and the great salvation, the gift of the Spirit brought with it, including the filling, completely apart from human merit. Apart from simple faith in Christ, there were no conditions that had to be met to receive spiritual completeness.

The Spirit, as He came, indwelt and baptized the disciples at Pentecost into Christ the moment they received the great salvation provided by Christ's work on the cross. God henceforth saw these believers *in Christ* and viewed them complete and perfect in Him as sharing His perfection and the completeness of His work in saving them.

The Pentecostal disciples were filled not because they waited and prayed for ten days. They were filled because they believed in the all-sufficiency of Christ's redemptive work and their completeness in Christ as a result of His salvation.

If the New Testament teaches us anything, it teaches that being filled with the Spirit is not a legalistic meeting of certain conditions. Such conditions as confession of sin, surrender to God, and prayer, are genuine and God-honoring only when they are expressions of faith in what Christ has done for us and what we are in Him. Always are they spurious when offered as works we do for God to gain merit.

The account of Pentecost (Ac 2) is one of the most abused portions of Scripture because the gift of the Spirit, the baptism of the Spirit, and the filling of the Spirit have been hopelessly confused in Pentecostalism, Neo-Pentecostalism, and similar charismatic movements popular at present.

The gift of the Spirit was the initial bestowment of the Spirit, inaugurating the new era and indwelling the church. At Pentecost the features of wind, fire, and tongues were designed to be strictly initiatory of the new age, not meant to be repeatable or to occur as normal features of the age once it was established.

R. A. Torrey, much quoted by charismatic leaders, mistakenly equated "the gift of the Spirit" with "the filling of the Spirit" and then identified both these terms with "the baptism of the Holy Spirit."[9] As a result, Torrey served "as a kind of John the Baptist figure for later international Pentecostalism."[10] The Pentecostal Donald Gee declares, "It was, perhaps, Dr. Torrey who first gave the teaching of the Baptism of the Holy Ghost a new, and certainly more scriptural and doctrinally correct emphasis. . . . His logical presentation of truth did much to establish the doctrine."[11]

Torrey's error comes to light when all the references to Spirit baptism are collated and the historical section is studied in the light of Jesus' upper room discourse and the doctrinal epistles.[12] Although the baptism and the filling at Pentecost occurred at the same time, this does not by any means indicate that they are always simultaneous nor that they are identical. Indeed, the reverse is true, as the study of chapter 2 has shown, by a six-fold contrast between the baptism and the filling.

The baptism and the filling could not possibly be the same. Although they may now as at Pentecost occur together with full and proper instructions beforehand, concerning positional fullness as the ground of experiential infilling, yet in the majority of cases, the filling occurs after the baptism and is repeated.[13]

The contrasting results accomplished by these two ministries of the Spirit at Pentecost will serve to emphasize the proper distinction to be observed between them. The result of the baptism appears in the pregnant words, "And the Lord added to the church" (Ac 2:47). Though the words *to the church* are not found in some of the oldest and best manuscripts, yet it was manifestly true that those who were being saved were being added to the church, as they are said to be "added to the Lord" (Ac 5:14). The Spirit was effecting this increase of the church, the body of Christ, invisibly by His baptizing work.

On the other hand, the results of the filling were remarkable and manifest—intense joy like "new wine" (Ac 2:13), intrepid boldness (2:14), divine power for witnessing and soul-winning (1:8; 2:41), steadfastness of doctrine, fervor of fellowship, persistency in prayer (2:42), unselfishness of heart (2:44), and the glow of ecstatic worship (2:47).

To maintain this high tide of spiritual life, continual fillings in the sense of adjustments to the control of the indwelling Spirit were necessary. This is why the Spirit came at Pentecost—to administer salvation and to enable the believer to be filled with the Spirit as a blood-bought privilege. It is not surprising, then, to read frequently of subsequent fillings (Ac 4:8, 31; 9:17; 13:9). Not once do we read of a subsequent baptism. The reason? The baptism puts us in Christ and in His body, the church, the sphere of the Spirit's indwelling. It must constantly be remembered that the baptism is the basis of the infilling, but *not* the experience of the infilling itself.

5. Pentecost marks the first historical occurrence of the baptism of the Spirit and the consequent formation of the church of Jesus Christ.

As A. C. Gaebelein correctly declares: "All believers were on that day united by the Spirit into one body, and since then, whenever and wherever a sinner believes in the finished work of Christ, he shares in that baptism and is joined by the same Spirit to that one body. . . . The believing company was then formed on the day of Pentecost into one body. *It was the birthday of the church.*"[14]

That there could have been no church, as the body of Christ, before that baptism, is just as certain as that it was impossible that there should not have been a church afterwards. This fact is evident from a simple comparison of Acts 1:5; 2:4; 11:14-16 with 1 Corinthians 12:13 and Ephesians 1:22-23.

"The church became an organism, that is, a living growing thing like a human body or tree. . . . As the Son needed a body through which to work, through which to obey, suffer, die, and rise again; so the Spirit needed a body through which to witness. At Pentecost He prepared Himself a body; He became incorporated. We think of the incarnation of the Son. I like to think of the transaction at Pentecost as the incorporation of the Spirit. The body He formed, He indwells, resides in."[15]

This very essential and fundamental truth that the church began at Pentecost is being controverted by two present-day errors. One of these maintains that the church existed before Pentecost (Mt 18:15-17).[16] Another holds that it was not formed till after Paul began preaching his distinctive message of grace.[17]

The church, however, could not have come into existence before the baptism with the Holy Spirit occurred, which was not until Pentecost (Ac 1:5; 11:15-16), because the body of Christ could only be formed by the Spirit's baptizing work (1 Co 12:13; Eph 1:22-23; Eph 4:4-5—"one body . . . one baptism").

Since Scripture places the first historical occurrence of the Spirit's baptism at Pentecost, it follows that the church was formed *then,* and not before nor after. What happened after Pentecost in the case of Samaritan (Ac 8) and Gentile (Ac 10) and under Paul's preaching (Ac 19:1-6) was the growth of the church, not its birth.

The church as the body of Christ could not have existed before the proclamation of the gospel of free grace embracing the death, burial, and resurrection of Jesus Christ. The disciples were strictly forbidden to preach or witness until they should receive the necessary spiritual equipment at Pentecost (Lk 24:49; Ac 1:8). The "church" of Matthew 18:17 is pre-cross and can only be thought of in the sense of *assembly,* according to the usage of the word in Acts 7:38 and 19:32. To construe the word *church* in the former passage as the body of Christ is to demonstrate a total lack of the biblical concept of the church (Eph 3:1-10).

The church could not have been formed when Jesus breathed on His disciples and said, "Receive ye the Holy Spirit" (Jn 20: 22). This was a unique and special incident. It met an exigency in the transition from one age to another, and in no sense formed the disciples into the mystical body of Christ.

Christ's imparting the Holy Spirit to the disciples was a sovereign act upon a chosen few to equip them for the ministry of the forty days (Ac 1:2-3). It was not performed upon the whole group to merge them into a corporate body. That could not take place until Christ had left the earth and sent the Spirit to regenerate, baptize, indwell, and seal the whole body, and grant the whole body the privilege of the filling by virtue of the indwelling Spirit. The Pauline revelation of the mystery (Eph 3) was the doctrinal foundation of the building of God (Eph 2:20-22) begun at Pentecost.

6. *Pentecost represents a new economy in God's dealing.*

The event followed the termination of the legal or Mosaic age, signified by the death of Christ and the tearing of the veil separating the holy place from the most holy place (Mt 27:51). A specialized ministry of the Spirit tided the disciples of Jesus over the fifty-day transition period (Jn 20:22), enabling them to comprehend Christ's *ad interim* teaching (Ac 1:1-3; cf. Jn 16:12-13).

This was the beginning of a new economy in God's dealing. The supernatural display of fire, wind, and tongues of Pentecost were the outward visible signals that the new age was being introduced. The Mosaic age had been inaugurated with fire, smoke, and earthquake as Mount Sinai was enveloped in flame (Ex 19:18). The future kingdom age will be inaugurated with signs of fire, smoke, and celestial commotions, accompanied by a phenomenal outpouring of the Spirit as at Pentecost (Joel 2:28-32; Ac 2:16-21).

Is it strange that phenomena of wind, fire, and tongues of various peoples should accompany the gift of the *Holy Spirit* to mediate Christ's salvation and to herald the gospel of grace to all nations? Modern charismatic movements overlook the important fact that Pentecost initiated a new age and that the initiatory aspects were once-for-all and unrepeatable.

The brilliant pyrotechnical display of languages (Ac 2:5-13) was a public demonstration that the new era being initiated—far from being confined to the Jew as in the Mosaic age—was to herald the outreach of the gospel to all humanity (Ac 1:8). This was of pivotal importance, since Pentecost was wholly Jewish. Non-Jews were not admitted to gospel privilege and membership to Christ's body till later: racially mongrel Samaritans were included in Acts 8:14-25; pure Gentiles, in Acts 10:1-48, perhaps as much as a decade after Pentecost.

Moreover, the tongues, wind, and fire were unmistakable signs to the Jews, showing them that God was doing a new thing. Because they had been inured to Mosaic legalism for fifteen hundred years, something unusual and spectacular would be required to shake them out of their religious traditionalism and awaken them to the fact that a new era in the divine economy was taking place.

As far as the Pentecostal tongues are concerned, they were due neither to the baptism of the Spirit nor the filling of the Spirit but to the giving of the gift of the Spirit and the inauguration of the new age.[18] They were the harbinger of the dominant feature of the new age, namely, world evangelization in fulfillment of our Lord's last words to His own before the ascension. "But ye shall receive power after the Holy Ghost is come upon you; and ye shall be witnesses unto me both in Jerusalem, and in all Judaea, and in Samaria, and unto the uttermost part of the earth" (Ac 1:8).

7. *Pentecost signals the opening of gospel opportunity to the Jew in a racial sense.*

To Peter Jesus had given "the keys to the kingdom of heaven" (Mt 16:19). This meant that to him would be delegated the authority to open the door of gospel opportunity at the beginning of this age. This he did to Israel on the day of Pentecost (Ac 2:38-42). That is why he was the God-chosen preacher for that day and the human instrument to proclaim to his Jewish hearers how they were to receive salvation through "the free gift of the Holy Ghost" (Ac 2:38).

It is to be observed that Peter was not given the keys of the church, but the keys of the kingdom of heaven as the sphere of Christian profession in the sense of Matthew 13. The Holy Spirit alone holds the keys of the church, as the sphere of Christian possession. He alone baptizes into that mystical body.

8. Pentecost bears a striking resemblance to Joel's prophecy of the latter-day outpouring of the Spirit inaugurating the kingdom age.

Peter had a purpose in introducing his Pentecostal sermon with a long quotation from the prophet Joel (Joel 2:28-32). He wanted to convince his multilingual Jewish listeners, gathered from all parts of the Roman Empire to celebrate the feast of Pentecost, that the strange exhibition of supernatural languages by the simple Galilean followers of Jesus was not an instance of drunkenness or mere emotional excitement. One of their own prophets had predicted similar spiritual phenomena to be visited upon their race prior to Israel's establishment in kingdom blessing.

It is obvious that Peter did not quote Joel's prophecy to claim its fulfillment in the events that had just taken place. The apostle purposely overquoted the passage beyond any possibility of its fulfillment then. He included events still unfulfilled, which would take place in the still-future day of the Lord preceding kingdom establishment (Ac 2:19-20).

Peter used the Joel passage as an illustration of the events of Pentecost. His phraseology "this is that" means nothing more than "this is [an illustration of] that which was spoken by the prophet Joel" (Ac 2:16). The fulfillment of this graphic passage in the time of Israel's restoration will consist not in the baptism of the Spirit, of which Joel knew nothing and which is confined to the church age, but in the indwelling and especially the filling of the Spirit "the pouring out upon all flesh" (Joel 2:28).

THE EVENTS AT SAMARIA AND THE BAPTISM OF THE SPIRIT

There are certain passages in the book of Acts which are employed to show that the gift of the Holy Spirit (erroneously called the baptism) is an experience after conversion. The present Scripture (Ac 8:4-25), commonly interpreted in a time and theological vacuum, is eagerly laid hold of to teach such a doctrine. Since the passage on superficial treatment seems to lend itself to such an interpretation, it is necessary to examine very carefully what took place and relate it to the baptism of the Spirit.

1. *The Samaritan revival marked the giving of the gift of the Spirit to the Samaritans.*

The gift of the Spirit—given, received, and permanently deposited in the church at Pentecost—is now, under the apostolic ministry of Peter and John, opened up to the Samaritans (Ac 8:4-24). At Pentecost the gift of the Spirit was received vertically (from heaven) in an age-inaugurating sense. At Samaria the gift as a permanent deposit of the church was dispensed horizontally (as an extension of the gift as a permanent deposit) to a unique racial entity as part of the gradual outreach of gospel privilege to the whole world (Ac 1:8).

The person of the Spirit (the gift), who arrived and took up permanent residence in the church at Pentecost, is now under apostolic ministry made available to Samaritans as the one who would bring them the gift of salvation and permanently indwell them. As Pentecost was an age-inaugurating event involving Jew or Jewish proselyte, the Samaritan revival marked the extension of the new era of salvation to the racially mongrel Samaritans.

As Pentecost introduced the common salvation of the new age to the Jew, the events at Samaria initiated the half-Jewish Samaritans into the same privilege. The occasion marked the admission of Samaritans into all the blessings of the Spirit, resident in the church since Pentecost, and now made available to them. This included *every* ministry committed to the Spirit in this present age: regeneration, baptism, indwelling, sealing, and the accompanying privilege of the filling.

It is obvious that the events at Samaria (as at Pentecost) do not represent something in addition to salvation, but the dispensing of the salvation of the new age itself. The Spirit of God in this inspired passage takes great pains to demonstrate this basic fact in a threefold way: first, by graphically describing Philip's revival; second, by highlighting the apostolic ministry of Peter and John; and third, by detailing the incident of Simon's deception.

The account of Philip's wonderful revival in Samaria is presented *not* to show that the Samaritans were already saved with the common salvation of the new age before the apostles' ministry to them. The whole point of the narrative is that *despite* their believing Philip's preaching "concerning the kingdom of God and the name of Jesus Christ" and their baptism in water "in the name of the Lord Jesus" (Ac 8:12, 16), they had *not* yet been admitted into the blessing of the gift of the Spirit.

Luke by inspiration *underscores* this pivotal point, the reason the Jerusalem church dispatched Peter and John to Samaria. They were to lay hands on the Samaritans that they might "receive the Holy Spirit" (Ac 8:14-16), that is, that they might be admitted into the new age and partake of its spiritual privileges. At Pentecost Jews had been admitted. Now racially mongrel Samaritans were let in. Later pure Gentiles would be granted entrance.

To emphasize how unique the situation was, Luke declares that the Samaritans had believed and been baptized in water with Christian baptism and yet had *not* received the Spirit. This plainly indicates that they were not yet admitted to the salvation the Jews had been admitted to since the Spirit's outpouring at Pentecost. "For not yet had [the Spirit] fallen upon any of them, but they had *only* [*monon*] been baptized into the name of the Lord Jesus" (Ac 8:16, paraphrased from the Greek).

That the Samaritans had been *only* baptized indicates that enough had not yet occurred, as indeed was the case. When the Samaritans received the Spirit by apostolic agency, they were initiated as a group into the new age, and that which was lacking was supplied. They received the Spirit, which means they were saved, as the Gentiles were when they received the Holy Spirit at Caesarea in the home of Cornelius (Ac 11:14).

After Peter and John had opened gospel privilege to the Samaritans, it was impossible for any Samaritan not to be saved, if he believed and was baptized in Jesus' name. The reception of the Holy Spirit meant that the gift given, received, and deposited in the church at Pentecost was now opened up and made available to others outside the Jewish race.

The terminology to "receive the Holy Spirit" *always* has an age-inaugurating connotation. Once Jew, Samaritan, and Gentile had been introduced to the gospel privilege of the new era, believers do not receive the Spirit.* When they believe on Christ, they automatically enter into the salvation made possible by the permanent, age-abiding deposit of the gift of the Spirit in the church. The instant the individual believes, the Spirit regenerates him, baptizes him into Christ and into union with all other believers, and enters the believer's body, which becomes a holy temple for the Spirit's permanent residence. In addition, the resident Spirit endows the believer with the privilege of the infilling of the Spirit, as the Spirit is allowed to control the believer's body (1 Co 6:19-20; Eph 5:18).

2. *The events at Samaria marked the opening of gospel opportunity to the Samaritans in a racial sense.*

There was real significance to the apostle Peter's coming to Samaria to pray for and lay hands on the Samaritan believers. At Pentecost, when gospel opportunity was made available to Jews in an ethnic sense, the ministry of Peter, as possessor of the keys of the kingdom of heaven (Mt 16:19) was necessary. Here for the same reasons appears the same apostle, aided by the apostle John (Ac 8:14-17).

The coming of the apostles was important in the divine plan to assure the authority and unity of the church. God saw to it

---

*Once the apostle Paul for the benefit of the legalistic Galatians employs the term "receive the Spirit" as tantamount to salvation (Gal 3:2). He does so to emphasize the gracious, completely unlegalistic character of the salvation the Holy Spirit, as the free gift of God, has mediated to believers.

that the Samaritan church did not arise independently from the Jewish church, particularly at the level of ultimate authority. Had this been the case, the ancient barriers of hatred and prejudice, so notorious between Jew and Samaritan (Jn 4:9) would have cradled the young church in schism at the commencement of its world outreach and mission.

The apostolic dispensing of the Holy Spirit to the Samaritans emphasizes the gospel in its grace, freedom, and universality. The salvation offered by the gospel is also as gracious, free, and universal. This is so because it is ministered by the free gift of the Holy Spirit outpoured by the crucified, risen, and ascended Saviour to *all* who believe. Even the despised Samaritans are not excluded. The only condition for the reception of the Spirit and the salvation He mediates for them, as for others, is simple faith in the redemptive work of Christ.

This is the principal purpose not only for the writing of the Samaritan event. It is also the reason for the account of the Gentiles' reception of the gift of the Spirit in Acts 10.

3. *The events at Samaria furnish a lasting warning to the making of conditions for God's free gift.*

There is a third featured event at Samaria (in addition to Philip's revival and the apostolic dispensing of the Spirit) which shows that the episode of Acts 8:4-17, as Acts 2:1-14, does not represent something in addition to salvation but the dispensing of the common salvation of the new age itself. This is the incident of Simon's deception (Ac 8:18-24).

Simon, like many charismatic believers today, was deceived into thinking that the free gift of the Holy Spirit, mediating a free salvation, could be obtained by paying a price, or by sacrifice rather than faith.

For example, the Pentecostal Riggs insists that prayer "is God's elimination test to determine whom He considers worthy to receive this priceless gift."[19] Barratt declares, "the more earnestly we covet a gift from God and the more we sacrifice to obtain it, the more we will prize it when it is obtained."[20]

Such views forget that God's salvation is *totally* free. Once the Holy Spirit had been given and deposited as a permanent gift in the church, it is salvation we receive. The indwelling of the Spirit is now the gift which has become a part of salvation and inseparable from it. The indwelling Spirit gives the privilege of the filling. The filling, too, is part and parcel of the free gift, enjoyed wholly by faith in what we are in Christ, not what we are in ourselves. It is based on what Christ has done for us, not what we do for Christ. Trying to be something or give something to obtain God's free gift is an insult to Christ's complete redemptive work.

Moreover, the baptism of the Spirit is not the gift of the Spirit. It is an inseparable part of the salvation the gift of the Spirit has bestowed.

Simon sinned against God by presuming to give God something for His gift. He supposed that one must pay a price for what God freely bestows. His background in sorcery and occultism (Ac 8:9-10) deluded him in seeking *beyond faith* to get possession of supernatural powers. He stands as a warning to those in the church today who dismember God's great gift of salvation and make any part of it contingent upon any condition other than simple faith in Christ's completed and fully efficacious redemption.

5

The Baptism of the Spirit at Caesarea and Ephesus

THE PROGRESSIVE REVELATION concerning the operation of the Holy Spirit in the new age inaugurated at Pentecost is seen in bold relief in the account of the events that took place at Caesarea (Ac 10:1-48; 11:13-18). Until this time gospel privilege—involving the free gift of the Holy Spirit—had been confined to Jew and Samaritan as racial entities. Now a new and startling development was about to take place.

Gentiles, unclean, so long shut out from religious opportunity, considered as "dogs" (Mt 15:24-27), symbolized by the various unclean animals of Peter's soul-transforming vision (Ac 10:9-16), were to be given the "like gift" that God gave the Jews at Pentecost (Ac 11:7) and the half-Jewish Samaritans (Ac 8:14-16). "Here the door was opened to the Gentiles and the first representative Gentile entered the church."[1]

THE GENTILE CORNELIUS AND THE BAPTISM OF THE HOLY SPIRIT

1. *The case of Cornelius marked the bestowal of the gift of the Holy Spirit upon the Gentiles.*

The events at Caesarea (Ac 10) stand in the same category as those that took place at Pentecost (Ac 2) and at Samaria (Ac 8). Each of these pivotal episodes is connected with the giving of the gift of the Spirit, thereby admitting a specific racial group into the spiritual privilege of the new era once it was inaugurated. That is why these events are high-lighted and given such prominence in the book of Acts. They are crucial to the correct understanding of the meaning of the term "the gift [*dōrean,* free gift, gracious present] of the Holy Spirit" (Ac 2:38; 8:20; 10:45; 11:17).[2]

Careful study of these key passages reveals that the term *the gift of the Spirit* has reference to the initial bestowment of the Spirit from the resurrected and ascended Christ upon Jew, Samaritan, and Gentile to work in them the great salvation purchased on the cross. At Pentecost the gift was given from heaven, received on earth, and permanently deposited in the church. This giving may be said to be in a *vertical* sense and was confined to Jew or Jewish proselyte.

At Samaria the permanently deposited gift was made avail-able to the racially mixed Samaritans, who were a bridge to the Gentiles. This giving was in a *horizontal* (not vertical) sense, in contrast to Pentecost. Though it was not age-inaugurating, it was age-extending. It opened up the spiritual privilege of the new age to others besides Jews.

At Caesarea the permanently deposited gift of the Spirit was extended to pure Gentiles. This dispensing of the gift of the Spirit was also in a horizontal sense, as at Samaria. With the extension of gospel opportunity to Gentiles, the inaugural features of the new age were completed and the normal course of the new era established.

The events at Pentecost, Samaria, and Caesarea as noted in the preceding chapter may be compared to the inaugural day of the American president. The period following this initiatory stage may be likened to the four-year term that follows the inaugural day. In terms of the illustration, the phrase *gift of the Spirit* is confined to the inaugural period. Once the gift of the Spirit was granted to Jew and Gentile, and the inaugural period ended, no longer was the Holy Spirit dispensed as a gift. The Spirit, now resident in the church corporately and in the believer individually, becomes the portion of the believer the moment he believes the gospel and is saved.

To be saved means this: the Spirit indwelling the church re-generates the sinner, baptizes him into union with Christ and with all other believers in Christ, enters his heart automatically to indwell him and to seal him as God's own. At the same time the Spirit offers the believer the privilege of continual infilling, as he allows the indwelling Spirit to control him.

Upon being saved, sinners do *not* receive the Holy Spirit. They believe on and receive Christ. In receiving Christ they are saved, which means the Spirit instantly moves into their heart to regenerate, baptize, indwell, and seal them, and endow them with the privilege of being filled (controlled) by the indwelling Spirit.

The terms *gift of the Spirit* or *receiving the Spirit* are therefore applicable solely to the introductory period of the church when the Holy Spirit was received from heaven (Pentecost) or the gift, received and deposited in the church, was introduced and made available to other racial groups, as the gospel was opened to them in its worldwide outreach.

2. *The bestowal of the gift of the Holy Spirit upon the Gentiles released the gospel of grace to the whole world.*

The giving of the gift of the Holy Spirit to the Gentiles at Caesarea (Ac 10:45), as in the case of Jews at Pentecost (Ac 2:38), and Samaritans under Peter and John (Ac 8:20), did not bring them something in addition to salvation, as Pentecostals and Neo-Pentecostals maintain, but salvation itself.[3] This could only be the conclusion because the free gift of the Spirit mediated a totally without-merit salvation proclaimed on the basis of the one true gospel of grace provided by the love of God through the finished redemptive work of Christ.

To construe the events in Cornelius' house as an experience subsequent to salvation (a so-called baptism equated with the Spirit's filling) and to attach conditions, is to deny the free gift of the Spirit, nullify the pure gospel of grace, and negate the absolute sufficiency of Christ's redemptive work on the cross.

The contention that Cornelius was saved before Peter's visit is invalid. He was a godfearing man, as indicated in Acts 10:2. But Scripture declares that he was not saved. Cornelius was told by an angel that Peter was to be summoned to tell him words by which he and all his house should "be saved" (Ac 11:14).

To contend that Cornelius was saved before the gift of the Holy Spirit was given to Gentiles is just as insubstantial as to argue that the disciples were saved prior to the giving of the Spirit to Jews at Pentecost or that the Samaritans were saved before Peter and John released the gift of the Spirit to them. The gift of the Spirit at Caesarea, as *always* in the book of Acts, "was no further experience, it was *the* experience of salvation. And this salvation was without conditions and 'without price'— it was simply given through the gospel."[4] (See also Gal. 3:2).

Moreover, this salvation administered by the bestowal of the gift of the Spirit through apostolic mediation brought with the Spirit's regenerating, baptizing, indwelling and sealing ministries the privilege of the infilling which the indwelling Spirit (the gift) now afforded.

Just as *no* Jew in the pre-Pentecost era enjoyed the so-great salvation that now in the post-Pentecost era comprises all these ministries of the Spirit, nor did any Samaritan before Peter and John introduced them to the gift of the Spirit, so no Gentile was saved until the gift of the Spirit released the common salvation of the new era to Gentiles in the home of Cornelius. Then and only then were the first representative Gentiles initiated into the gospel and the salvation it brings to everyone who believes.

Now that the age has been introduced to all mankind, everyone enters into the blessing of the outpoured gift of the Spirit the moment saving faith in Christ is exercised. Moreover, it is of the utmost importance to remember that "the final order for this age . . . was not established until the experience in Cornelius' house."[5] As the normal course of the new era was attained with the bestowal of the gift of the Spirit upon the Gentiles, a point of immense significance was reached. The gospel of grace, based on the crucified and risen Redeemer (1 Co 15:1-4), was now opened up and made available to every creature under heaven.

3. *The bestowal of the gift of the Spirit upon the Gentiles established the proper relation between Spirit baptism and water baptism.*

The normal order of the age indicates that the water ceremony is inseparably connected with the spiritual reality it reflects and should follow it as soon as possible. Peter's words are highly significant. "Can any man forbid water, that these should not be baptized, who have received the Holy Spirit as well as we?" (Ac 10:47). Since the reception of the Spirit by the Gentiles initiated them into salvation and not something in addition to salvation, it was to be followed by believers' baptism. This alone is Christian baptism, which always presupposes Spirit baptism as a vital and inseparable component of salvation mediated by the gift of the Spirit.[6]

At Pentecost the outpoured gift of the Spirit of course mediated the same salvation to Jews who believed. There, too, Christian baptism is directed to *follow* salvation. When Peter on that occasion instructed Jews convinced of sin how to be saved, he said, "Repent, and be baptized, everyone of you, in the name of Jesus Christ for the remission of sins [*i.e.* exercise saving faith] and ye shall receive the gift of the Holy Spirit [*i.e.* you shall be saved]" (Ac 2:38).

Peter, of course, was not making any conditions for salvation beyond simple faith in Christ. Repentance and baptism in Jesus' name were simply the *evidences* of saving faith and receiving the gift of the Holy Spirit was salvation. Peter's gospel in Acts 2:38 is the same as Paul's gospel in Ephesians 2:8-9: "For by grace are ye saved through faith; and that not of yourselves: it is the gift of God: not of works, lest any man should boast."

At Samaria baptism in Jesus' name definitely preceded the giving of the gift of the Spirit and the salvation it brought to the Samaritans (Ac 8:12, 14-16). But the narrative presents this circumstance as a complete abnormality. Why? Because the Spirit "as yet was fallen upon none of them; only they were baptized in the name of the Lord Jesus" (Ac 8:16).

Never after the gift of the Spirit had been given, opening up salvation to the Samaritans, could this order ever occur again. The reason is simple. In this age water baptism, as a witness to the inner work of grace, always follows the spiritual reality and pictures Spirit baptism. The latter is a vital and inseparable part of salvation and its unique feature during this age. It unites the believer to Christ and to all who are in Christ. In this way it differentiates the salvation purchased by Christ on the cross from pre-cross salvation that looked forward to the cross.

Scripture closely connects Spirit baptism and water baptism. The connection both in the book of Acts and in the epistles is in fact apparently so close as to form the "one baptism" of the church (Eph 4:5). Nevertheless, Spirit baptism (the spiritual reality) is also clearly differentiated from the water symbolism (the ritual ceremony). Apart from Spirit baptism, the water ceremony is meaningless and in no sense to be thought of as Christian baptism at all. The one represents the position and experience of salvation, since Spirit baptism is a vital and inseparable part of salvation. The other symbolically portrays that salvation as a witness and testimony to others that one has already been saved.

Water baptism then can add nothing to a completed salvation. It merely witnesses to the reality of that salvation before men, and graphically pictures union with Christ by virtue of the Spirit's baptizing work (1 Co 12:13; Ro 6:3-4; Gal 3:27; Col 2:8-10).

4. *The bestowal of the gift of the Holy Spirit upon the Gentiles clarifies the purpose of tongues in the book of Acts.*

Tongues in the book of Acts were in every instance a sign (2:4; 10:46; 19:6). Specifically they were a sign to Jews *only,* never to Gentiles. At Pentecost the supernatural languages (with the wind and fire) constituted a tangible demonstration of the introduction of a new divine economy. The transition from almost fifteen centuries of Mosaic legalism to the new era of grace (Gal 3:23-29) was so earth-shattering that the Jew required undeniable evidence that the change-over was really God's doing (cf. 1 Co 1:22).

The Pentecostal tongues (known languages supernaturally given) were a divine token that the Spirit had come from heaven to take up His permanent residence in the new people of God on earth. They signified that the gift of the Spirit was given by the ascended Lord and received on earth and deposited in the new people of God to perform His ministries for the age in working in the believer Christ's glorious salvation purchased on the cross.

At Caesarea as at Pentecost the sign of supernatural language (Ac 10:46) was connected with the inauguration of a new age. Pentecost opened the inaugural phase. The events at Caesarea closed it and marked the attainment of the *normal course* of the new era. Tongues were a witness to the Jews of this fact. Peter and the Jewish witnesses who accompanied him to Caesarea were fully assured by divine intervention that the new age had been fully introduced and its normal order set with the outgoing of gospel privilege to the Gentiles.

Even more important, the phenomenon of languages supplied a much-needed demonstration to the Jews that the gift of the Spirit (salvation) granted to Gentiles was in every sense equivalent to the gift of the Spirit poured out upon them at Pentecost. The Jews needed incontrovertible evidence, not only that God had given the gift of the Spirit to Gentiles, but that it was "the like gift," equal in every sense to His gift to the Jews (Ac 11:17). So evident was the demonstration of this that Peter could report to the Jews at Jerusalem, "Forasmuch, then, as God gave them the like gift as he did unto us . . . who was I, that I could withstand God" (Ac 11:17).

At both Pentecost and Caesarea the sign of tongues was unconnected with either the baptism of the Spirit or the filling of the Spirit. Tongues were the age-initiating token of the giving of the gift of the Spirit and the harbinger of the thrilling fact that the great salvation the Spirit was to work out was to be for all humanity. As the supernatural languages suggested, this salvation was to be broadcast in every tongue of man to every tribe on earth through the gospel of grace.[7]

In connecting tongues with the baptism of the Spirit (also erroneously called the filling) instead of with the age-inaugurating gift of the Spirit, modern charismatic Christians make a basic mistake. They are forced to attach various conditions to what is an inseparable part of God's free gift and totally by God's grace. In addition they are misled to attach a sign to the giving of the gift when the sign was only applicable to its bestowment upon Jew and Gentile in the beginning in an age-initiating sense.

Once the age was opened, the sign of its opening was no longer needed. Tongues in Acts were a sign to Jews collectively. Never were tongues a sign to individuals except as individual Jews are viewed as members of their racial or religious group. This fact is of the utmost importance in understanding the purpose of tongues in the book of Acts.[8]

"Speaking in tongues in Acts is on all three occasions a corporate, church-founding, group-conversion phenomenon, and never the subsequent Spirit-experience of an individual."[9] Both at Pentecost and at Caesarea glossolalia was "unsought, unexpected, and undemanded. . . . In Acts, on the three occasions where tongues occur, they come to an entire group at once . . . bringing complete Christian initiation . . . and occur apart from recorded effort on the part of the recipients."[10]

THE EPHESIAN DISCIPLES AND THE BAPTISM OF THE SPIRIT

One more misunderstood passage in Acts has been made the source of unsound teaching. This is the episode of the twelve disciples of John the Baptist who became New Testament believers (Christians) under the gospel of grace proclaimed by Paul (Ac 19:1-6).

On the surface, and especially in the misleading rendering of the original Greek in the Authorized Version, the passage might appear to teach that receiving the Holy Spirit is an experience subsequent to salvation. This is a superficial conclusion which can only be corrected by a thorough study of the immediate context of the event (Ac 18:24—19:7) in the light of the other key passages in the Acts, namely, Pentecost, the Samaritan revival, and Cornelius' conversion.

1. *The Ephesian disciples knew nothing of the giving of the Holy Spirit and the ministries He undertakes in this age for every believer.*

The spiritual status of these dozen men was substantially the same as Christ's disciples before Pentecost, the Samaritan believers before Peter and John ministered to them, and Cornelius and the Gentiles before Peter came to Caesarea. In other words the Ephesian disciples were not saved (Ac 11:14) with the common salvation of the new age before Paul preached to them the gospel of grace and free salvation. When he did so, they entered into the blessing of the outpoured gift of the Spirit, now a permanent deposit of the church, and became Christians.

The situation of the Ephesian disciples, however, was different from the Jews at Pentecost or the Samaritans or the Gentiles at Caesarea. They had not "received the Holy Spirit" (Ac 19:2)—not because they belonged to a race to whom the Holy Spirit had not yet been given, introducing the gospel of grace and the common salvation of the new age. The sole reason was they did not know that the Spirit had come and that the gift had been given and received and was now a permanent deposit of the church. They did not know that the new era inaugurated at Pentecost had been introduced to both Samaritans and Gentiles and had now for some time been established in its normal course.

These twelve Jews (or conceivably Jewish proselytes) had no knowledge whatever of Pentecost or its meaning—that the Spirit had been given to them as a race and a new age begun. This fact is obvious from their reply to the apostle Paul when he inquired if they had received the Holy Spirit. "But we did not so much as hear that the Holy Spirit *is*" (Acts 19:2 from the Greek, italics added).

This same idiom occurs in John's gospel to elucidate Jesus' prophecy of the Spirit to be outpoured at Pentecost. "If any man thirst, let him come unto me, and drink. He that believeth on me, as the scripture hath said, out of his belly shall flow rivers of living water." John's comment is, "But this spoke he of the Spirit, whom they that believe on him should receive:

for the Holy Spirit *was not yet* [from the Greek, italics added] because that Jesus was not yet glorified" (Jn 7:37-39).

To summarize: (a) Before Pentecost, "The Holy Spirit *was not yet*" (Jn 7:39); (b) at Pentecost, "The Holy Spirit came, arrived, and took up residence"*; (c) after Pentecost, "The Holy Spirit *is*" (Ac 19:2).

These disciples, some twenty-odd years after the Holy Spirit had been given at Pentecost, were still living, insofar as their knowledge and experience were concerned, in the pre-Pentecostal era. They were evidently regenerated, but what is certain is that none of John's disciples could be said to have been baptized, indwelt, or sealed with the Holy Spirit (Ac 1:5). Hence what happened to the Ephesian group spiritually was not something in addition to salvation, but (as at Pentecost, Samaria, and Caesarea) salvation itself.

When the Ephesian disciples reposed faith in Christ, the Holy Spirit baptized them into Christ's body, the church, and into Christ Himself. He indwelt them, sealed them, and also powerfully filled them, as a token of their introduction to the privileges of the new age. (Apparently they were already regenerated, as were the Old Testament saints.) All this is meant in the phrase, "The Holy Spirit *came on them*" (Ac 19:6; cf. Ac 2:4).

In all this there is not the slightest basis for the idea of a second blessing. The apostle's question to them was whether they had received the Holy Spirit *when* they believed (19:2). The Authorized Version, "Have you received the Holy Ghost since ye believed?" is very misleading. "The two aorists point to one definite occasion."[11]

A. T. Robertson lists this passage as an example of "the coincident aorist participle, which follows the verb,"[12] and expressing "simultaneous action."[13] The translation of the Revised Version is, therefore, correct: "Did you receive the Holy Spirit when ye believed?" This accurate rendering removes any ground for the erroneous notion that the Spirit was received at some time subsequent to the exercise of saving faith.

*See Chapter 4, "The Baptism of the Spirit at Pentecost and at Samaria."

2. *Tongues at Ephesus were a sign to the Jews that salvation was now possible for their race only on the basis of faith in Christ's redemption ministered to them by an outpoured Spirit.*

Like their teacher Apollos, the Ephesian disciples knew only John's baptism. Apollos, though "mighty in the Scriptures," that is, he knew the Old Testament, "knew of no baptism but John's" (Ac 18:25, Weymouth). Like him (19:3), they consequently knew only of the baptism with water "unto the remission of sins" (Mt 3:11). This is clear evidence that they were completely ignorant of the baptism with the Holy Spirit, except as a prophesied event (19:4). For all they apparently knew, it was still future as in the days of John's prediction of it. They knew nothing of it and the gift of the Spirit that brought it and the great salvation of which it is a vital part.

Indeed, it seems the Ephesian disciples were Jews or "Jewish proselytes, disciples of John, looking for a Coming King, not Christians looking back to an accomplished redemption."[14] Paul, who proclaimed the gospel of grace to these disciples, was himself a "Hebrew of the Hebrews" (Phil 3:1-10), a glowing example of the truth he brought to them. They on their part were vivid illustrations of the fact that now the Jew as well as the Gentile, as a sinner, was wholly shut up to faith in Christ for salvation.

Could it possibly be true that those who clung to the teachings of Judaism so long into the new age could be shut out of the great salvation purchased by Christ's death and ministered by an outpoured Spirit? The incident at Ephesus gives a ringing answer. Yes! Religious Jews must come the same way as unreligious Gentiles.

Faith in the coming One (Ac 19:4) could no longer avail. The coming One had arrived, purchased His great salvation on the cross, died, rose again, and ascended to heaven, pouring out the gift of the Spirit to work in the believer His great salvation. Knowledge of John's baptism (Ac 19:2) could no longer suffice. The preparatory ceremony had given way to the spiritual reality. The baptism of the Spirit had become effective as a vital part of salvation, ministered by the outpoured gift of the Spirit.

In the light of these facts, the apostle Paul preached the gospel of grace to the Ephesian disciples of John and Apollos. He proclaimed Jesus Christ and a completed redemption (Ac 19:4-5). He expounded the message of grace and the salvation it brought, mediated by the free gift of the Holy Spirit. They were baptized with Christian baptism. "And when Paul had laid his hands upon them, the Holy Ghost came on them; and they spoke with tongues and prophesied" (Ac 19:6).

The tongues, as at Pentecost and at Caesarea, were a sign to the Jews. They were not related, as has been seen, to some experience subsequent to salvation, as modern charismatic leaders contend, but to the dispensing of the common salvation itself, which the new age offered through the outpoured gift of the Spirit. Specifically they were a divinely attested token that salvation was now possible for the Jew, no matter how dutiful to Judaism, only on the basis of Christ's completed redemption ministered by an outpoured Spirit.

3. *The conversion of the Ephesian disciples illustrates the importance of sound doctrine for faith to lay hold of and for experience to be tested.*

The important consideration with regard to the Ephesian disciples was not whether they had believed, as this is plain, but *what* they had believed. The object of faith is just as vital as faith itself. Faith can be folly if it is directed toward the wrong object. The object of their faith was faulty. Similarly modern charismatic movements do not lack faith but rather accurate doctrinal truth for faith to take hold of.

The message of John, introductory and purely preparatory, was now antiquated and superseded. Faith in it could not bring the free gift of the Spirit as the blessing of the new age and the new message of salvation based upon Christ's redemptive work. The moment the Ephesian disciples heard and received the new message, they received the blessing of that message—salvation mediated by the gift of the Holy Spirit.

It is always perilous to be doctrinally careless or irresponsible. Believing a false gospel can deprive one of salvation. Believing error can distort one's experience. Genuine spiritual experience can result only from faith in sound biblical teaching. The hazard of subscribing to popular teachings on the baptism of the Holy Spirit as a second experience evidenced by glossolalia is that the believer leaves the safe ground of God's Word. When one does this, there is no safeguard against the intrusion of spirits not from God (1 Jn 4:1) to spoil the true work of the Holy Spirit in the believer's life and experience.

6

The Baptism of the Spirit in 1 Corinthians, Romans, and Galatians

THE BAPTISM of the Spirit was predicted in the gospels and historically realized in the Acts. It was doctrinally defined in the epistles. In second-blessing theology and twentieth-century charismatic movements, interpretations placed upon the historical sections have not always harmonized with the teachings of the doctrinal epistles. However, when the historical accounts are viewed in their proper time perspective, they are in perfect agreement with the doctrinal epistles.

Six passages from the epistles refer to the baptism of the Spirit: 1 Corinthians 12:12-13; Romans 6:3-4; Galatians 3:27; Colossians 2:10-12; Ephesians 4:5; and 1 Peter 3:21. Of these, the Corinthians passage is the most important, both because it clearly refers to Spirit baptism and it treats the subject comprehensively.

THE BAPTISM OF THE SPIRIT IN FIRST CORINTHIANS 12:12-13

To the apostle Paul was given the distinctive revelation of the church as the body of Christ formed by the Spirit's baptizing work. His writings reveal the doctrine, position, walk, and destiny of the church. In his epistles the baptizing ministry of the Holy Spirit—predictive in the gospels, and historic in the Acts—finds its full doctrinal expression.

1. *Baptism as used by Paul in connection with the Holy Spirit has the distinctive meaning of bringing the believer into organic union with Christ through power capable of effecting a vital change in the believer.*

To understand the significance of Spirit baptism, one must see this wider meaning of the Greek terms *baptō* and *baptizō*, meaning to baptize. It may be called the mechanical usage and refers to real baptism, the inner spiritual reality. It stands in distinction to the ceremonial usage, referring to ritual baptism, the outward water ceremony, reflecting and witnessing to the prior accomplishment of the inner spirtiual transaction.*

That this broader meaning of baptism—to bring into organic union or under the power of anything which is capable of effecting a change—comes down from ancient times is exhaustively demonstrated by Dale. In answer to the question of what is classic baptism, Dale's reply is this: "Whatever is capable of thoroughly changing the character, state, or condition of any object is capable of baptizing that object and by such change of character, state, or condition, does in fact baptize it."[1]

It is not surprising, therefore, to read of baptism *into* repentance (Mt 3:11), baptism *into* the name of the Father and of the Son, and of the Holy Spirit (Mt 28:19), baptism *into* Moses (1 Co 10:2), baptism *into* Christ (Gal 3:27), *into* His death, *into* His burial (Ro 6:3-4), and baptism *into* His body (1 Co 12:13).

The Israelites were baptized into Moses by the cloud and by the sea. In this way they were separated from Egypt and Pharaoh, came under the leadership of their deliverer, and identified with him in hope and destiny. Likewise the believer, by being baptized into Christ by the Spirit, is cut off from the world and Satan, and identified with Christ, coming under Christ's influence and control, and made one in hope and destiny with Him.

The baptism of the Spirit, accordingly, brings the believer

---

*For full discussion, see Chapter 7, "The Baptism of the Holy Spirit in Ephesians."

into organic union with the body and under the imputed merits and power of Christ, the Head. This means the believer is united to Christ and to *all* other believers joined in this manner to Christ. "For as the body is one, and hath many members, and all the members of that one body, being many, are one body: so also is Christ" (1 Co 12:12).

As a branch to a vine, and as a member to a body, this divine baptism establishes an identity between the believer and his Lord, and a unity with all other believers in the Lord. This union is indicated in the many passages which declare that the believer is in Christ. In fact, so wonderful is this identity and union between the believer and his Lord and all other believers joined to the Lord by this divine baptism, that the apostle calls the spiritual body formed "the Christ" (1 Co 12:12).

By the term *Christ* in this passage the apostle does *not* mean the literal Christ in glorified humanity seated at the right hand of the Father in token of His finished redemptive work. The reference is to the mystical Christ—Christ in heaven united eternally by the Spirit's baptizing work to His redeemed people on earth.

2. *The baptism of the Spirit is the ground of the oneness of all believers in Christ.*

How could the apostle more emphatically underscore this great truth than by using the figure of the human body (1 Co 12:12-26)? One body has many members and functions. But it is *one* body, not two or more. The repetition in verse 12 and 13 is highly significant "The *body is one . . . one body . . . one body.*" The comparison is even more significant—"so also is the Christ."

Satan and demonic powers have always been arrayed in deadly opposition to Christ, both when He was upon the earth in the days of His flesh and now as He, the Head in heaven, is upon the earth in the mystical form of His body, the church—joined to His people and His people to Him—by the Spirit's baptizing work. This is the reason for the Satanic and demonic onslaught against the unity of the church, the body of Christ, through false doctrine and resulting division (1 Ti 4:1). This attack has been persistent down through the centuries. But it is being intensified as the end of the age nears (2 Ti 3:8-16).

Anticipating Satan's attack upon the oneness of the Lord's people, Paul penned this passage to warn against division. "That there should be no schism [rent or split] in the body, but that the members should have the same care one for another" (1 Co 12:25; cf. 1:1-12). Believers are to resist error, especially concerning the truth of Spirit baptism as the ground of their unity, ever remembering they "are the body of Christ, and members in particular" (1 Co 12:27; see also Eph 5:30).

Schism today threatens the body of Christ in a dangerously camouflaged form, disguised as a deeper spiritual experience. This is seen in the Pentecostal division of baptism. One baptism is into Christ for all believers; another spiritual baptism is into the Spirit, reserved for a special category of Christians who meet certain conditions and demonstrate certain evidences. But a movement which begins by violating the concept of *one* spiritual baptism (Eph 4:5), so plainly set forth by the apostle in this passage, cannot avoid the Satanic snare of dismembering the one body and dividing the fellowship of Christians.[2]

As if anticipating modern confusion, the apostle purposely made his chief objective in his first letter to the Corinthians to emphasize the oneness of all believers as constituting the body of Christ, joined to the Head, and forming the mystical Christ Himself. He addressed the Corinthian believers as those who "are sanctified in Christ Jesus, called . . . saints" and hastens to add, "with *all* who in every place call upon the name of Jesus Christ, our Lord, both theirs and ours" (1 Co 1:2). In the introductory passage of the epistle he stresses *that* which *all* the saints at Corinth have "in Christ Jesus" (1 Co 1:2-11).

It is as if the apostle took special pains to ward God's people away from any Satanic lure to tempt them to subscribe to false teaching that would violate the one spiritual baptism, destroy ing the unity of God's people that is grounded in it. Actually the attack on the unity of God's people "in Christ" is an attack on Christ Himself in His mystical form as joined to His people by the Spirit's baptizing ministry.

3. *The agent of the baptism of the Spirit is the Spirit Himself.*

The baptism which the apostle describes doctrinally is pointedly the baptism "by" and "with" the Spirit. The Authorized Version is accurate. "For by [*en*] one Spirit were we all baptized into one body." The reference is patently to the very common instrumental use of the Greek preposition *en* indicating agency, translated "with" or "by" or "by means of."[3] The same baptism "by" or "with" (*en*) the Spirit (instrumental case) occurs in the other references to the baptism of the Spirit (Mt 3:11; Lk 3:16; Ac 1:5; 11:16). The reference in Mark 1:8 *without* the preposition is instrumental.

It is often objected that 1 Corinthians 12:13 must be rendered "in the Spirit" (locative case of sphere) because the verb is passive and the agent is personal (the Holy Spirit). But Paul evidently intentionally preserved the wording found in the other references to Spirit baptism, listed above, where John's *with-water* baptism is contrasted with Christ's *with* or *by means of* Spirit baptism. Also, the apostle uses the Greek preposition *en* to express instrument or agency with a passive verb and a personal agent in 1 Corinthians 6:2, 11: "The world shall be judged *by* [*en*] you," and you are "justified *by* [*en*] the Spirit of our God."

The rendering "in" or "in the sphere of" the Spirit (locative of place) adopted by many scholars still indicates Spirit baptism. This is true even if water baptism is introduced. For the water ceremony is only valid Christian baptism as it reflects and symbolizes the *previous* Spirit baptism which it portrays.

In the face of this plain scripture declaration concerning Spirit baptism that *every* believer when he is saved is so baptized, charismatic theology is forced to posit a second spiritual baptism. Various exegetical gymnastics are attempted to evade the doctrinal finality of this passage. One such attempt tries to maintain a distinction between being baptized *by* the Spirit (1 Co 12:13) and being baptized "in" or "with" the Spirit (the passages listed above in the gospels and Acts). On the basis of this contention, it is granted that while *all* believers are baptized *by* the Spirit when saved, they still need to be baptized *in* or *with* the Spirit *by Christ,* as a subsequent experience. This latter second spiritual baptism, it is claimed, is what is referred to in the passages on Spirit baptism in the gospels and Acts. However, such a distinction based on the Authorized Version—which employs the preposition *with* in the gospels and Acts and *by* in 1 Corinthians—has no basis in the Greek. The preposition is the same in *all* cases, and the spiritual baptism referred to, one and the same.[4]

It is conclusive, therefore, that 1 Corinthians 12:13 presents the Spirit as the agent of the baptism. As the Pentecostal gift, since His original bestowment to be the permanent deposit of the church (Acts 2) and to be personally resident in the body of Christ, the Spirit baptizes every believing sinner into the one body, the precise moment he is saved, *never* subsequent to the exercise of saving faith.[5]

4. *The baptism of the Spirit is universal among believers.*

The universality of this spiritual baptism, wrought for all God's people in this age, without a single exception, leaves no room for believing it is a second spiritual experience enjoyed by only a part of God's people. "For by one Spirit are we *all* baptized into one body." The same all-inclusiveness stressed so emphatically in the Corinthian passage is likewise indicated in the expressions: "Ye . . . all," "as many of you" (Gal 3:26-27), "so many of us" (Ro 6:3).

The inescapable truth taught by the apostle is that the one Spirit baptizes all—every believer—into the *one* body and that there is only *one* body. That which is wrought by the Spirit is an inseparable part of the believer's salvation, "else it could not include each one."[6] Indeed it could not be otherwise, for all the genuinely saved in this age are "in Christ," and no one can attain this position apart from the baptizing ministry of the Spirit.

5. *The baptism of the Spirit makes possible the filling of the Spirit.*

Placed by one Spirit into the one body, the church, the believer is introduced into the sphere where the fullness of the

Spirit is possible because the Spirit Himself resides in the one body collectively and in each member of it individually. The metaphor of filling pictures the indwelling Spirit as a fountain from which the believer may drink until he is filled.

Spirit baptism transfers the believing sinner from the waterless desert, where he faces imminent death by thirst, and places him in an oasis of life. But it does more than this. In the oasis it sets him beside a never-failing fountain of refreshing water, even putting a cup into his hand, so that he may drink until filled, and drink and drink again and again, as he may have need.

This is the picture the apostle presents of Spirit baptism in the latter part of 1 Corinthians 12:13. The result of being baptized by one Spirit into the one body is that *all* believers at the moment they were saved were "made to drink into one Spirit." They were given the privilege by virtue of their position in the body, the church, and in the mystical Christ Himself (1 Co 12:12), to drink to the full of the Spirit.

The latter half of verse 13, again in the aorist tense in the Greek, supplements the former half by emphasizing that the Spirit *at the same time* He baptizes all Christians into the one body of Christ places them in the sphere of spiritual (positional) fullness. Because they are in Christ, God sees them as Spirit-filled. He thus grants them the privilege of experiencing his fullness. This does not mean that the baptism of the Spirit is the experience of the filling of the Spirit, as is so popularly but erroneously supposed in current charismatic confusion. It does mean, however, that the baptism guarantees spiritual fullness which is the basis of the filling, but is not itself the experience of the filling.[7] In other words, positional fullness makes possible experiential fullness, but it is not in itself experiential fullness.

Likewise, experiential fullness (that is, consistent infilling of the Spirit) has no other condition than simple faith. But in this case the faith is not that of the sinner who believes that Christ died for him. It is rather that of the saint who believes he died in Christ—died to sin that he might live to righteousness (Ro 6:11). Being filled with the Spirit is not on the basis of legalistic requirements and human conditions, signifying what I can do or ought to do for God. It is rather the gracious, free appropriation of what Christ has done for me and what I am in Him. This puts both positional fullness and experiential infilling where they belong—in Christ, not in ourselves—in God's great salvation, not in something in addition to it.

Confusing the baptism of the Spirit with the filling of the Spirit is why modern charismatic movements obscure the true gospel of grace and do violence to God's free gift of salvation. Unwittingly introduced is essentially a form of Galatian legalism, in which the all-sufficiency of Christ's redemptive work is set aside and some form of human merit or works is introduced into the saving process.[8]

Even more serious, confusing the baptism of the Spirit with the fullness misleads believers into the Colossian heresy,[9] in which the completeness of the believer in Christ (by the Spirit's baptizing work) is denied. As a result something in addition to salvation (being "in Christ") is added and required. This makes part-fullness, part-power and part-life in Christ in the face of the apostle's sublime declaration: "In him dwelleth all the fullness of the Godhead bodily. And ye are complete in him" (Col 2:9-10).

6. *The baptism of the Spirit is unique among the Spirit's ministries.*

Oneness of the believer with the Lord is emphatically "by *one* Spirit . . . into *one* body" (1 Co 12:13) by *"one* baptism" (Eph 4:5). The agent of the union is unique—one Spirit. The result of the union is unique—one body. The operation by which it is accomplished is unique—one baptism.

The duration of the operation is unique. The baptizing work of the Holy Spirit is the only ministry of the Spirit confined to this age. It is distinctive to the formation of the church, the body of Christ. When this particular group of God's elect is completed and called out of the world, there will be no longer any need for the baptizing work of the Spirit, and it will terminate.

Perhaps the most unique feature is the result of the Spirit's baptizing work—the one body. No other operation can accomplish what the baptism of the Spirit does. By it is formed the mystical Christ (1 Co 12:12), the risen glorified Christ in heaven joined to His redeemed body on earth by the Spirit's baptizing work. As a result all believers are not only in Christ, they *are* the (mystical) *Christ*.

For this reason it is apparent that the unique spiritual baptism of 1 Corinthians 12:13 is the baptism that is in view in those passages that speak of or imply organic union with Christ, such as Romans 6:3-4; Colossians 2:12; Ephesians 4:5; and Galatians 3:27. Spirit baptism, accordingly is explicit in these great passages. Water baptism is *implicit* in them only and strictly as it reflects and outwardly attests the already accomplished spiritual reality it is meant to portray. Otherwise the water ceremony is completely irrelevant and has no connection whatever with Christian baptism.

THE BAPTISM OF THE HOLY SPIRIT IN ROMANS 6:3-4

In the letter to the Corinthians the apostle deals with the baptism of the Spirit as a joining of the believer to the body of Christ, and hence to Christ Himself, the head of the body. This is the positive aspect of baptism—organic union. But there is a negative aspect as well. There must first be a *separation from* before there can be a *joining to*. In Romans the apostle deals with the negative aspect of the Spirit's baptizing ministry by way of introduction to the positive aspect.

1. *The baptism of the Spirit disconnects the believer from his position in Adam.*

In Romans 5:12-21, the passage which introduces the apostle's teaching on Spirit baptism and its connection with a holy life (Ro 6:1-23), the sinner in his lost condition "in Adam" and the saint in his saved state "in Christ" are contrasted. The sinner is set forth as being in a positon under condemnation springing from one man, Adam (Ro 5:12, 15, 18). The saint enjoys justification, with all condemnation removed, issuing from one, the last Adam (Ro 5:14).

Condemnation is shown to be universal in its extent upon all in the old creation under Adam's federal headship (Ro 5:12-17). Similarly justification is declared to be universal in its extent to all "in Christ" in the new creation (Ro 5:18). Condemnation in the old creation in Adam entails judgment, which is due (Ro 5:16). Justification in the new creation in Christ secures the free gift of eternal life, whch is not due (Ro 5:16-17). Condemnation abounds in the old creation in Adam (Ro 5:20). Justification superabounds in the new creation in Christ (Ro 5:20).

By this contrast of the sinner in the old creation and the saint in the new, the apostle shows that the believer has been cut off and completely removed from his former position under sin and condemnation "in Adam" by the baptizing work of the Spirit and placed "in Christ" (Ro 6:3-4) in a new sphere of justification and righteousness. "All the details of his salvation spring from this new position."[10]

By the term *position* is meant the sphere in which God sees the justified sinner who believes on Christ. The Spirit of God takes the believing sinner out of his lost estate in Adam at the moment of salvation and places him eternally in Christ. In this new placement the Father views the justified believer in the merits and perfections of His Son. He henceforth sees him always and only as "accepted in the Beloved" (Eph 1:6), simply because he *is* in the Beloved.

In this new estate, the Father declares to every one of His sons—strictly by virtue of their unchangeable and unforfeitable position in His only begotten Son—what He declared to the latter at His baptism, "This is my beloved Son, in whom I am well pleased" (Mt 3:17).

2. *The baptism of the Spirit identifies the believer with Christ.*

Being cut off from Adam, the believer is free to be joined by the Spirit to Christ. In 1 Corinthians 12, the baptism of the Spirit is viewed as bringing the believer into the body of Christ. In Romans 6 the inseparable truth is presented, that baptism also places the believer *in Christ Himself.* This great truth had already been anticipated in Corinthians. There the apostle compares the body of Christ not only to the human body, but to the mystical Christ Himself (1 Co 12:12)—Christ in heaven joined to His body, the church, on earth.

As a result of the new position the believer receives when he is saved by the Spirit's baptizing work, he by virtue of this transaction comes into possession of all the elements of his salvation. This includes justification, sanctification, deliverance, access to God, inheritance and glorification. Failure to undertand the far-reaching ramifications of Spirit baptism has nurtured many false doctrines and robbed many believers of assurance and the joy of their salvation.

This is notably true in twentieth-century charismatic trends. Modern Pentecostals, for example, believe that the baptism of the Spirit—rather than being positional and nonexperiential and constituting an inseparable part of salvation—is an experience subsequent to salvation. Moreover, they believe it is a dramatic, critical experience. Anything less experiential than the baptism in water by John the Baptist, charismatic leaders feel, fails to do justice to what they imagine the term to mean.[11]

In contrast to such a view, the baptism of the Spirit in Romans is presented as uniting *all* believers to Christ in a position of identification and inseparable oneness with the crucified and risen Saviour in the experiences of His death, burial, and resurrection. "Know ye not, that so many of us as were baptized into Jesus Christ were baptized into his death? Therefore, we are buried with him by baptism into death: that like as Christ was raised up from the dead by the glory of the Father, even so we also should walk in newness of life" (Ro 6:3-5).

By means of the baptizing work of the Holy Spirit in this pivotal passage, putting the believer "into Christ" and in this way identifying him with his crucified and risen Saviour in the experiences of His death, burial, and resurrection, a fulfillment of Jesus' strange reply to the ambitious request of James and John, to sit at His right and left hand in His kingdom, finds an explanation. "Ye know not what ye ask: Can ye drink of the cup that I drink of? and be baptized with the baptism that I am baptized with? . . . Ye shall indeed drink of the cup that I drink of; and with the baptism that I am baptized withal shall ye be baptized" (Mk 10:38-39).

The cup to which our Lord enigmatically referred was plainly the cup of God's wrath against sin shortly to be pressed to his sinless lips, and for the sake of guilty sinners, drained to its bitter dregs by Him "who knew no sin," but who was "made . . . sin for us . . . that we might become the righteousness of God in him" (2 Co 5:21). The baptism, which is inseparably linked with the cup, is unquestionably His baptism into death, which He accomplished by the shedding of His blood.

But how could James and John drink the cup that Jesus drank and be baptized with His baptism of death? By identification with their crucified and risen Lord through the Spirit's baptizing work.

In Romans 6 all believers, including James and John, are seen to be identified with Christ's very death, buried with Him, and raised again with His very life. Through the believer's union with the risen Christ there is a real sense in which he was with his Lord on the cross, his lips drinking the terrible cup of God's wrath against sin and dying with Him. This is the resplendent truth upon which Romans 6 is based. It is the great fact to which the apostle refers elsewhere, notably in Galatians 2:20: "I have been crucified with Christ; and it is no longer I that live, but Christ liveth in me" (ASV). It is the theme of the grand old Negro spiritual that rings with poignant pathos:

Were you there, when they crucified my Lord?
Were you there, when they crucified my Lord?
Oh! Oh! sometimes it causes me to tremble, tremble, tremble!
Were you there, when they nailed Him to the tree?

3. *The baptism of the Spirit is symbolized and outwardly attested by water baptism.*

Some teachers correctly differentiate the baptism of Romans 6:3-4 from water baptism. However, they unwarrantedly distinguish it from Spirit baptism, making it a separate "baptism into death" in contrast to the Spirit's baptizing work, which is supposed to be a "baptism into life."[12] But this differentiation is wholly unnecessary. The Spirit first places the believer in the sphere of Christ's death that he might be the beneficiary of Christ's glorious resurrection life. Moreover, baptism into the body of Christ (1 Co 12:13) is an initiation into the experiences of that body (Ro 6:3-4), which in turn are the experiences of Christ Himself, the Head and Saviour of the body (Eph 1:20-23; 5:23).

On the other hand, because the glorious spiritual realities dealt with in Romans 6 are such as no ritual ceremony could possibly effect, and because the truth of identification with Christ must already have been an actuality in the experience of the convert before the water ceremony could be administered, it is quite evident that the ritual ordinance is no more under explicit consideration in Romans 6:3-5 than in other key passages on Spirit baptism (1 Co 12:13; Col 2:10-12; Gal 3:27).

Here as elsewhere water baptism bears a relationship to Spirit baptism. It portrays outwardly and symbolically what Spirit baptism has already affected inwardly and vitally by uniting the believer to Christ and identifying him with the Saviour in death and resurrection. Water baptism, in other words, is symbolic—either of the cause or means of union with Christ, as many Christians hold, or the effect or result of that union, as others believe. As such the water ceremony always underlies the spiritual reality.

At any rate, properly understood in its scriptural relation to Spirit baptism, water baptism is divinely intended to be a symbol of unity, a portrayal of the oneness of all believers in their common relationship, first to Christ and secondly to one another in Him. It is meant to be a reminder that this unity is effected by the baptizing work of the Spirit.

The unhappy results of the church's misconception of this symbol of unity, distorting it into a device for disunity, is well stated by Walvoord:

> It is a sad reflection in the church's spiritual discernment to observe the historic emphasis upon the sacrament without

recognition of the baptism of the Holy Spirit which it should represent. In human hands the sacrament has become a divisive force in the Church instead of the portrayal of the unity of the body of Christ and its identification with Christ. How important and how precious is the truth that the believer is in Christ Himself with all that this position entails.[13]

4. *The baptism of the Spirit is the basis of a holy walk.*

The problem of sin in the believer lay behind the apostle's exposition of the baptism of the Holy Spirit in Romans 6 as identification with Christ. This same problem has vexed Christians in all ages. John Wesley advanced second-blessing perfectionism. Charles G. Finney preached a baptism of the Spirit subsequent to salvation. Holiness movements posit second-experience sanctification. Modern Pentecostals promote a second spiritual baptism in the Holy Spirit evidenced by tongues.

But all must go back to Paul. The apostle solved the problem once and for all. He set forth the only sound solution—*not* second-blessing perfectionism, *not* a subsequent-to-salvation spiritual baptism, *not* some after-salvation experience of sanctification, *not* a baptism in the Spirit signified by tongues. Identification with Christ through Spirit baptism is the only solution, declares Paul.

The apostle states the problem in Romans 6:1: "What shall we say then? Shall we continue in sin that grace may abound?" In answer he outlines the believer's identification with Christ through Spirit baptism as the basis for victory over indwelling sin (Ro 6:2-10). Paul is careful to point out that this spiritual baptism is not a second experience for some, but the position of all believers and the ground for holy living as saints.

This spiritual position means the believer died to sin (v. 2), because he has been bapitzed by the Spirit into organic union with Jesus Christ. He is accordingly identified (made one) with Christ in death (vv. 3-5). Because the believer died (with Christ), he is set free from sin, the old man, the man as he was in Adam, corrupt and depraved. Having thus died when Christ died, the believer is as a result no longer "in Adam," his old position of sin and condemnation, but "in Christ," his new position of righteousness and justification before God (vv. 6-7). Consequently, since the believer is also identified with Christ in resurrection, he is the recipient of resurrection life and power to live in victory over sin (vv. 8-10).[14]

In verse 11 the problem of sin in the believer is solved by a key. The key is that of faith. It enables the believer to convert his glorious unchangeable position before God into a corresponding experience and consistent practice before men. To open the door of doctrinal truth contained in verses 1-10 to practical experience requires two turns of the key of faith: one negative—"reckon ye also yourselves to be dead indeed unto sin"; the other positive—"but alive unto God."

The Greek is very emphatic. "You reckon" (*logizesthe*), "keep on counting as true," "keep on believing" that you are what you are in Christ, taken out of your old position of sin in Adam, and placed in a new position of righteousness in Christ. The point the apostle would have us see is that the believer is "dead indeed unto sin" and "alive unto God" because he is in Christ Jesus by virtue of the baptism of the Holy Spirit. The difference is that when the believer knows this and believes it, it becomes experientially real.

This is the crux of the problem of holiness in the life of the believer. The baptism of the Spirit is the ground of it. Faith is the key to it. It is not some experience after salvation. It is the experience of salvation itself, as the Holy Spirit works it out in response to faith. As faith continually counts on what we are as identified with our Lord, the believer is enabled to convert his glorious unchangeable position in Christ into a glorious experience of Christ.

Christ then manifests Himself in and through the Christian. This and this alone is true Bible holiness. Any other variety that counts on what one is in himself, even to the slightest degree, rather than on what one is in Christ, is false.

THE BAPTISM OF THE SPIRIT IN GALATIANS 3:27-28

In Galatians, as elsewhere in Paul's epistles, the truth of the union and identification of the believer with Christ, so fully expounded in 1 Corinthians and Romans, is taken as the basis of *all* the believer's positions and possessions in Christ (Gal 2:20; 3:1-5, 27, 28; 5:6, 24; 6:15).

1. *The baptism of the Spirit is a spiritual coming of age and a liberation from legalism.*

"For as many of you as have been baptized into Christ have put on Christ" (Gal 3:27). Since the Spirit's baptism is here identical with the truth expressed in the figure "have put on Christ," and not merely concomitant with it, as the Authorized Version might lead us to believe, it is better to follow the American Revised Version: "For as many of you as were baptized into Christ did put on Christ."[15]

The figure of dress is undoubtedly borrowed from contemporary life. The Greek or Roman youth upon passing from boyhood to manhood marked the important transition by a change of dress from the boyish tunic to the adult male toga. The youth had been subject to domestic rules and regulations, but he now passed out of this preparatory stage into the privileges and responsibilities of citizenship.[16]

The baptism of the Spirit (in a dispensational sense) is then a spiritual coming of age. The believer in the Mosaic era was bound to obey definite commandments and fulfill specific duties. Now by virtue of new spiritual privileges he comes of age. As a result he is set free from the rules which governed him as a child under the law. He is liberated to heed the inner voice of the Spirit and to discharge by the Spirit's supernatural enablement the weightier obligations of a citizen of a heavenly commonwealth. He now has the opportunity to avail himself of the gracious privileges which are his as placed in vital relationship to Christ.

The baptism of the Spirit is, accordingly, a "putting on Christ." This means the believer as a result of Spirit baptism is transported from the immature stage of legalism into the adult stage of faith in Christ. In this position the believer is clothed with Christ's own standing and merit. He rejoices in perfect acceptance by virtue of a finished redemption. No longer, as under the Old Covenant, does he labor to be accepted by the performance of legal minutiae. Nor does he fulfill certain conditions to obtain spiritual fullness, except as that fullness resides wholly and completely in Christ and is received solely by faith in Christ's finished redemption.

The very meaning of the baptism of the Spirit as the coming of age spiritually and the liberation from legalism was being threatened by the legalizing teachers at Galatia. The apostle in the Galatian epistle masterfully demonstrates that "Christ hath redeemed us from the curse of the law" by becoming "a curse for us . . . that we might receive the promise of the Spirit through faith" (Gal 3:13-14).

The false teachers at Galatia were attempting to introduce special laws and conditions of obedience in order to bring about a greater removal of sin to procure the full gift of salvation. Paul shows that such laws and conditions, besides denying Christ's redemption from all forms of legalism, were not restraints against sin, but positive incentives to sin, because of the weakness of the flesh. If men are to be set free from sin, they must not be saddled with laws. They must be liberated from them (Gal 2:18-19; 3:19). This is the liberation Christ purchased in His redemptive work, which the false teachers were nullifying, besides sowing superficial concepts of sin.

The apostle shows what modern-day Pentecostals need to know, that adherence to the law does not procure the Spirit. The gift, given at Pentecost and permanently deposited in the church ever since, is mediated in a free salvation humanly conditioned by faith in Christ alone. It is the Spirit who sets the believer free from the law. The fulfillment of the just requirements of the law takes place miraculously by God's power, *not* by man's efforts, conditions, and toned-down views of sin.

When the gospel of grace is believed and not violated, the divine order in the believer's history becomes release-fulfillment. When *any* form of Galatian legalism is imported, the gospel of grace is perverted and the divine order set aside. Substituted is the reverse order fulfillment-release, the usual mystical or spiritualistic formulation and expectation. This becomes in reality a denial of the absolute all-sufficiency of Christ's death for the mediation of the gift of the Spirit. "But if righteousness is through [any kind of] law, then Christ died for nothing" (Gal 2:21, from the Greek).

2. *The baptism of the Spirit is received wholly on the basis of faith.*

This fact must be so, because the Spirit's baptizing ministry is a vital and inseparable part of salvation, which is "by grace . . . through faith," totally apart from works and self-effort (Eph 2:8). The precondition of the giving of the gift of the Spirit was the redemptive work of Christ, releasing the believer from the law (Jn 7:37-39; Gal 3:10-14; 4:4-7). To enter into the benefits of the Spirit, as the permanent deposit of the church, faith must be exercised in the redemptive work of Christ. The result of such faith is the free gift of salvation wrought in the believing sinner by the Spirit.

The believers in Galatia were being turned aside from the message of faith to law keeping. "You foolish Galatians, who has bewitched you, before whose eyes Jesus Christ was publicly portrayed as crucified? This is the only thing I want to find out from you: Did you receive the Spirit by the works of the Law, or by hearing with faith? Are you so foolish? Having begun by the Spirit, are you now being perfected by the flesh?" (Gal 3:1-3, NASB).

The Galatians were being threatened with an error that finds expression today in second-blessing holiness movements and in Pentecostalism. They were being led to expect the Holy Spirit in greater measure through some means other than the simple message of faith that brought them salvation and the indwelling Spirit. They were being "bewitched" by the attractive appeal of a *fuller* gospel with *fuller* conditions of obedience bringing a *fuller* salvation.

The apostle, of course, does not oppose obedience to the commandments of God or exemplary conduct. What he does contest, however, is any obedience except that which springs out of faith centered in what Christ has done for us and what we are in him. This stands in stark contrast to reliance upon what we do for Christ and what we are in ourselves as the basis of a full relationship to God.

One of the great featured truths of the Galatian epistle is that God's constant and full supply of the Holy Spirit, and of the miracles which are part and parcel of the life in Christ, are gifts given not only in the very beginning of the Christian life through the unconditioned message of faith in Christ (Gal 3:2) but richly and fully supplied throughout the Christian career on the very same basis of faith, totally apart from works (Gal 3:5).

To make the baptism of the Spirit a subsequent experience is to dismember salvation, of which it is an inseparable part. To attach conditions to it, other than simple faith in Christ, is to repudiate the apostle's teaching and espouse the role of the Galatian legalizers. To go back to legalistic rules and regulations as prerequisites for relationship to God is to put off the adult dress with which faith in Christ clothes us and to go back to the childhood dress and the legalistic restrictions of a former age. Modern second-blessing holiness movements and twentieth-century Pentecostalism must face the issues involved.

3. *The baptism of the Spirit rightly understood guards the true gospel against perversion.*

Believers who realize that by the Spirit's baptizing work in salvation they have been placed eternally and securely in Christ and as a result have "put on Christ" (Gal 3:27) are able to see the true gospel of grace and hold to it against all contamination and perversion. The Galatian believers were being drawn away from this great truth. As a result they, like many of their modern Pentecostal and second-blessing holiness brothers, were falling from grace (Gal 5:4). This meant they were being removed from "the grace of Christ unto another [*heteros*] gospel" (Gal 1:6).

The apostle does not use the Greek word for "another," *allos,* which means of the same kind, but the word *heteros,* not of the same class or category. In reality it is a false gospel, and hence not the gospel at all, only a perversion of it (Gal 1:7). In this solemn passage the apostle "finalizes and fixes the true gospel of redeeming grace from any admixture of legalism or human works."[17]

Paul's somber *anathema* sounds a note of warning in a day of charismatic confusion and the proclamation of other gospels, including the so-called full gospel. The latter term is common in Pentecostalism and is based in part upon the conviction that it is with the alleged Pentecostal baptism in the Holy Spirit that the Spirit is given fully or that one receives full salvation.

It is quite apparent that this claim is a variation of the Galatian heresy that brought forth the apostle's stern charge of another or false gospel. The "full gospel" is based upon the fallacy that the common salvation purchased by Christ on the cross is not complete when initially received by faith. It must be added to by an additional experience in which certain conditions are met or standards of holiness attained.

This is the very alluring error appealing to our human energies, similar to the one by which the Galatians were "bewitched" (Gal 3:1). It forgets what the apostle points out in the Galatian epistle. Salvation purchased on Calvary is always full, never partial or piecemeal. It is, moreover, always ministered by the one true gospel of grace and is identical in content for all believers. Therefore it is called "the common salvation" (Jude 3). The gospel does not admit of the designation full or not full, but only true in contrast to false.* The full gospel of certain holiness groups turns out, under the apostle's stern definition, to be a false or at best a perverted gospel.

The true gospel declares what Christ has done for us and what we are in Him totally by God's grace. It calls for knowledge of this great free salvation and the exercise of faith and faith alone to make it real in our experience—not only at conversion but continually in the experience of progressive sanctification (cf. Ro 6:11; Gal 2:20).

Yieldedness to God, prayerfulness, separation from sin, or any other actions on the part of the believer are *not* conditions or legal requirements of self-effort. They are rather privileges the grace of God grants to us and are the responses of faith in what we are in Christ, not in anything we are in ourselves.

The perverted gospel of the Judaizers in Galatia did not offer

*See chap. 1, fn. 24.

its conditions and legal requirements as substitutes for the gospel but merely as expletives, things added to fill out the gospel, and which foster the modern idea of "full gospel." This is substantially the case with Pentecostal and many holiness groups today.

These Christians, of course, do not deny the deity or Saviourhood of Christ. But they do often deny the security of the believer in Christ. They do hold that the gospel is sufficient for the beginning of the Christian life, but not for its continuance. They do believe the gospel brings the Holy Spirit initially but not fully. They do maintain the sinner is saved initially by grace through faith, but must do or not do certain things to keep saved.

But most important of all, they have the idea that pure grace and faith are not sufficient for the realization of the fuller, deeper, victorious, Spirit-filled life. This, they think, calls for them to do something or be something in themselves in the way of meeting certain conditions, taking certain steps, or obeying certain laws (as at Galatia). Meanwhile, all the gospel requires them to do is simply this: To keep in mind what Christ has done for them in uniting them eternally to Himself and to count on (believe) this glorious position by freely and spontaneously making the proper response of faith.

This response of faith will mean a dedicated life, a Spirit-filled life, a victorious, prayerful, triumphant life—*totally apart from human conditions and fleshly activity*. This is exactly why in the Galatian epistle the apostle Paul insists upon the all-sufficiency of the true gospel for the beginning, the continuing, and the fulfilling of the Christian life.

4. *The baptism of the Spirit produces a unity transcending all human relationships and distinctions.*

The apostle explains in the letter to the Galatians that the new age of spiritual adulthood introduced by the outpoured Spirit has completely superseded the old age of spiritual immaturity with its rules and regulations. On this basis Paul repudiates every claim, whether based on law or any other principle, of any distinct class or superior sanctity in Christ.

The baptizing work of the Spirit, making all believers one in Christ Jesus, does away completely with all distinctions of race, social status, and sex, which were characteristic of the legal age. "There is neither Jew nor Greek, there is neither bond nor free, there is neither male nor female: for ye are all one in Christ Jesus" (Gal 3:28).

Under the Mosaic law a sharp line was drawn between Israelites and non-Israelites. Only to the Jew "pertaineth the adoption, and the glory, and the covenants, and the giving of the law, and the service of God, and the promises" (Ro 9:4). In Christ this distinction is discarded (Ro 10:12; Eph 2:13-16; Col 3:11). Under the law legal barriers and social change severed freemen from slaves. In the body of Christ such differences disappear (1 Co 7:20-24). Even such natural divisions as deep-rooted as those of sex, which figured so prominently under the Mosaic economy, are unrecognized in the organic unity of believers consummated by the Spirit's baptizing work (Ac 1:14).

In the light of the marvellous unity of the body of Christ effected by the Spirit's baptizing work, how little the apostle would tolerate present-day divisions among God's redeemed people caused by charismatic confusion. How deeply he would deplore the schisms occasioned by glossolalic movements. How thoroughly he would denounce separating the Lord's people into two groups—one merely saved and the other a class of supersaints getting a so-called full salvation.

If ever the church needed the corrective teaching of the epistle to the Galatians, it is at the present hour. God help the saints to see what the true gospel is and the glorious free salvation it brings to all who believe.

7

The Baptism of the Spirit in Ephesians, Colossians, and 1 Peter

THE EPISTLE to the Ephesians reaches a high-water mark of revelation concerning the position and the possessions of the believer as the result of his in-Christ relationship. Since Paul is not writing to the Ephesians to correct doctrinal error, he is free to devote his letter to a magnificent exposition of the believer's position in Christ. Since this position is accomplished by the Spirit's baptizing ministry, the epistle in its entirety is really a commentary on the baptism of the Spirit.

The Colossian epistle, while also referring to Spirit baptism (2:8-10), does so in the context of correcting certain dangerous errors. Since these same errors are prominent in our day, and spring from wrong views of Spirit baptism in relation to Christian position and experience, the epistle is extremely vital to understanding the current charismatic scene. The first epistle of Peter also adds significant light on the subject of Spirit baptism so needed in contemporary Christianity.

THE BAPTISM OF THE SPIRIT IN EPHESIANS 4:5

The results of the Spirit's baptizing work form the warp and woof of the teaching in the Ephesian letter. The believer's position in Christ receives full exposition, together with the possessions and experiences of Christ this wonderful position guarantees the child of God. Despite the fact that the baptism of the Spirit underlies the entire argument, there is only one

117

direct mention of this momentous operation in the epistle itself. This occurs in chapter 4:5.

1. *The one baptism of Ephesians 4:5 is Spirit baptism.*

This reference, however, has frequently been denied classification as Spirit baptism. It is sometimes interpreted purely as water baptism. Often it is construed in a sacramental sense as a Spirit-water combination, marking the critical point at which God's salvation enters the individual life, when faith in the gospel becomes public in the water ceremony.[1] This view is common in current New Testament scholarship and represents a variation of newer Baptist views.[2]

The chief objection to this sacramental view is that it teeters perilously on the precipice of the error of baptismal regeneration. It cannot conceivably avoid declaring that faith in Christ's redemptive grace is not sufficient for salvation. It rather affirms that the gospel of grace is faith in Christ plus water baptism rather than faith in Christ plus nothing.

Water baptism is always implicit in the explicit New Testament references to Spirit baptism and is always an outward portrayal of the inward spiritual realty. It is a testimony to one's faith in Christ, with the spiritual transformation involved. But this is quite different from attaching sacramental efficacy to the waters of baptism.

It is impossible for the sacramental view not to cast a cloud upon the glorious all-sufficiency of Christ's atoning work on the cross and make some human work or act of obedience necessary. Is water baptism "the *place* where God identifies the believer with Christ and his work"?[3] Or is it the foot of the cross where the penitent sinner trusts Christ? Does the Spirit place the believer in Christ the moment he believes or does He wait until the believer is sprinkled, poured upon, or immersed in water? What about unbaptized infants who die in infancy? If water baptism is the *place* where God identifies believers with Christ, instead of the cross, many true believers would never be joined to Christ.

Much more important, the epistle to the Ephesians denies the doctrine that water baptism is "the *place* where God identifies the believer with Christ and his work." According to the epistle, salvation is by grace through faith plus nothing (Eph 2:8-9). This salvation comprehends being placed in Christ* by the Spirit's baptizing work. This position includes being "blessed with all spiritual blessings . . . in heavenly places *in* Christ" (1:3), "chosen . . . *in* him before the foundation of the world" (1:4), made "accepted *in* the beloved" (1:6), "*in* whom we have redemption" (1:7), "have obtained an inheritance" (1:11), and "were sealed with that holy Spirit" (1:13), having been raised up "together in heavenly places *in* Christ Jesus" (2:6).

That the "one baptism" of Ephesians 4:5 is the baptism of the Spirit is demonstrated by the context. This passage deals with spiritual truths, not ritual ordinances.[4] The apostle lists seven spiritual truths which form the doctrinal foundation for Christian unity: one body, one Spirit, one hope, one Lord, one faith, one baptism, and one God (Eph 4:4-5).

The one body is, of course, Christ's body, the church, composed of all believers baptized by the Holy Spirit into Christ (1 Co 12:12-13; Ro 6:4-5). The one Spirit is the Holy Spirit, who alone can baptize the believer into organic union with Christ and unite him with *all* other believers in Christ. The one hope is the blessed (joy-imparting) expectation centering in Christ's return for His own and their resurrection and glorification in Him (Titus 2:13).

The one Lord is our Saviour, Christ Jesus. He is the originator of Christian oneness by virtue of His redemptive work and consequent role as the giver of the gift of the Spirit and baptizer with the Spirit (Mt 3:11; Mk 1:8; Lk 3:16-17; Jn 1:33; Ac 1:5; 2:33). After His bestowment of the Spirit as the exalted Redeemer at the right hand of the Father, the Spirit given, received, and deposited in the church on earth became the baptizer (1 Co 12:12-13).

The one faith is that essential body of Christian revelation "once for all delivered to the saints" (Jude 3). The one bap-

*An expression used or implied more than a score of times in this epistle alone, which is addressed to those "in Christ Jesus" (Eph 1:1), see 1:3, 4, 6, 10, 13, 23; 2:5, 6, 10, 13, 21, 22; 3:12; 5:8; 6:1, 10.

tism is Spirit baptism, the only means of union with Christ
(1 Co 12:12-13). The one God is the "Father of all, who is
above all, and in you all."

Let it be repeated that although water baptism symbolizes
Spirit baptism and is meant to be an outward testimony, it is
not under consideration in Ephesians 4:5. Naturally the apostle
makes no declaration concerning that which the context clearly
indicates is not under discussion. Neither is he implying that
because there is only one baptism, water baptism is not to be
practiced during this age.

2. *Spirit baptism is the doctrinal basis for Christian unity.*

The apostle Paul's far-reaching doctrine of the church as the
body of Christ (1 Co 12:13) finds full treatment in the
Ephesian letter (Eph 1:22-23; cf. Ro 6:3-5). The great revelation of Ephesians is that Christian unity is not something
man concocts and brings about by human strategy and ecumenical fervor. Christian oneness is a reality. God Himself
has brought about unity, and His people are to recognize it as
the teaching of His Word and realize it by appropriating faith.

Christ prayed for the unity of His people in His great high
priestly prayer, uttered before His death on the cross (Jn 17:11,
20-21, 23). His petition was answered in His death, resurrection, ascension to the Father, and the giving of the gift of the
Spirit. The Spirit came to minister Christ's salvation. An important part of that great salvation is the work of the Spirit
in baptizing believers into Christ and bringing them into vital
union with one another in union with Christ.

This doctrinal basis of the unity of all believers is set forth
in detail in the first three chapters of the epistle to the
Ephesians. "Hitherto, under Paul's trusty guidance, his cru-
saders have been treading the loftiest passes of revelation, ab-
sorbed in the panorama of a massive mountain-chain of Christian doctrine. . . . Now it is time for them to descend from
these craggy altitudes . . . to the lower levels of everyday duty
and demeanor; from the *credenda,* in short, to the *agenda;* for
all doctrine truly held prompts to corresponding practice."[5]

Begining at Chapter 4 the question arises, how can this doctrinal basis of Christian unity be translated into the realization and practice of unity among Christians? The apostle indicates two steps to be taken. First there must be a walk on the part of each individual Christian which will be consistent with his exalted position in Christ (Eph 4:1-3). The doctrine of the oneness of believers in Christ by the Spirit's baptizing work is a spiritual doctrine and can only be realized experientially on the basis of spirituality.

That the practical realization of Christian oneness is possible only on the basis of the high spiritual vitality of the various members of the body of Christ is why so little unity is manifested. The oneness of God's people is so often denied, ignored, or misconstrued, and false bases and man-made organizations are substituted for the unity of the Spirit.[6]

But the unity of the Spirit is only possible in experience because of the oneness in position of *all* God's people accomplished by the baptizing work of the Spirit. Moreover, unity must rise out of doctrinal purity. Only genuine revival based on God's Word can make Christians really forget sectarian divisions and unite them in practical oneness. Thus, a second step toward the realization of Christian unity is a correct understanding of the biblical basis of Christian oneness (Eph 4:4-6). This step requires understanding revealed truth (doctrine), while the first step deals with faith to put that doctrine into practice.

Scripture reveals that the unity of God's people is based upon the seven spiritual unities: one body, one Spirit, one hope, one Lord, one faith, one baptism, and one God. Liberals who deny these basic unities can erect only a false ecumenical structure that is as flimsy as a house built on sand. But Pentecostals, Neo-Pentecostals and second-blessing holiness Christians who misconstrue the one (spiritual) baptism cannot possibly help unify. The very ground of that unity is removed by their two spiritual baptisms which produce two bodies of believers, instead of the one spiritual baptism, producing only one body in which all believers are united in Christ by the Spirit's baptizing ministry.

Neither can orthodox, Bible-believing Christians be instrumental in experiential unity unless their doctrine is translated into experience by faith. Dead orthodoxy is as much at fault for schism in the body as live heresy. There can be no practical realization of the truth of the oneness of God's people in Christ without faith producing a consistent walk. Truth must be joined to faith, and faith must be joined to truth. Only then can the Lord's people enjoy the oneness that is their rightful heritage in Christ.

3. *The baptism of the Spirit correctly understood is one of the most edifying and unifying doctrines of Scripture.*

It is for this reason that Paul includes Spirit baptism among the seven great spiritual verities to be clearly understood. Only then is it possible for Christians to enter into the benefits of Christian unity.

To remove the interminable strife, the sectarian divisions, the doctrinal schisms, the petty jealousies, and the factional antagonisms so common among Christian people today, the church must catch a clear vision of the Spirit's baptizing work uniting *all* believers to Christ. This vision could remove the error of substituting ritualism for reality, and church membership for a salvation experience.

If believers could see the greatness and completeness of their salvation, they would begin to cooperate with the Spirit to work out in their lives what He has already worked in their hearts (Phil 2:12-13) instead of seeking some experience of the Spirit in addition to salvation, one not authorized by the Word of God.

In the age of the occult and the latter-day era of increased demonic activity (1 Ti 4:1-2; 1 Jn 4:1-2; 2 Th 2:6-12), spirits not of God are waiting to delude and give transcendental experiences that are a dime a dozen in pagan religions. Correct understanding of Spirit-baptism would center the believer in his position in Christ. There alone is he safe from demon attack, as he claims what he is in Christ and stands his ground on the Word of God. This is the only place of immunity against the delusive attack of powerful demonic forces as the end of the age advances.[7]

Moreover, in view of the unifying effect of the doctrine of the one body by the one Spirit and the one baptism, it is clear the apostle could not intend the one baptism to refer merely to water baptism. In striking contrast to Spirit baptism, the water rite has been a notoriously disunifying factor from the very beginning of church history. As a sacrament or ordinance it is observed in various forms and with the most diverse interpretations. By a few it is not observed at all. Although it has its proper place and meaning, it is a far cry from the operation indicated by the apostle in Ephesians 4:5.

THE BAPTISM OF THP SPIRIT IN COLOSSIANS 2:9-12

The apostle's reference to Spirit baptism in Colossians complements the revelation contained in Romans. The thought of identification with Christ is paramount in both epistles. However, in Colossians special emphasis is placed upon Christ's burial. And the burial of our Lord is an important element of the gospel (1 Co 15:4). It demonstrates the certainty and finality of Christ's death and of our death to sin as united to Him.

In addition to special emphasis on certain aspects of identification with Christ, Colossians gives important revelation concerning the baptizing work of the Holy Spirit in relation to the believer's position in Christ and to his spiritual circumcision. In Romans the baptism of the Spirit is presented as the basis of a holy walk. In Colossians it is laid down as the foundation of a heavenly walk.

1. *The baptism of the Spirit makes the believer complete in Christ.*

Christ is complete in His deity: "For in him dwelleth all the fulness of the Godhead bodily" (Col 2:9). And the believer is complete in Christ: "And ye are complete in him" (Col 2:10).

The range of the word *complete* as used with reference to the believer is beyond human understanding. Nevertheless, the Holy Spirit declares that as God sees and evaluates things according to His divine standards, the child of God is complete in Christ. There is *nothing* to be filled out or to be added to the believer's salvation. It is finished and perfect, so that the believer, as far as God sees him as united to Christ, has no lack or deficiency whatever. He is perfect in his unchanging *position,* just as the Saviour into whom he has been baptized by the Spirit is perfect.[8]

To what, it may be asked, is such a transformation due? The answer is clear. It is due to Christ's finished redemptive work providing such a great salvation (Heb 2:3) ministered by the outpoured gift of the Spirit. But specifically it is the result of the Spirit's baptizing ministry, one of the vital and inseparable elements of this great salvation, by which the believer is placed in union with Christ. In this new sphere, the believer partakes of all Christ's perfection and merit before God!

The believer is complete because he is in Christ. He is in Christ because he is baptized into union with Him by the Holy Spirit. Being in this way identified with Christ, he partakes of all that Christ is. And what is Christ? He is the delight and perfection of the Father (Mt 3:17). By the believer's union with the Son, the believer likewise becomes the delight and perfection of the Father. While men in general are accounted mere creatures of God's hand, alienated from the Creator and undone by the fall, those who are saved are, even now, perfected in the Father's sight because of their vital union with the Son.

It is apparent that by the baptizing work of the Holy Spirit a principle is introduced that is as glorious in its implications for the believer as it is beyond the grasp of the unbeliever. This principle becomes the basis of all the positions and possessions that measure the riches of divine grace.

In Colossians the principle involves being complete in him (2:10); in Ephesians possessing all spiritual blessings in the heavenly places in Christ (1:13); in Romans being positionally already glorified in Him (8:30); in Philippians having citizenship in heaven (3:20); in Corinthians being workers together with God (2 Co 6:1).

The blessings belonging to the child of God because of his union with Christ through the Spirit's baptizing work in salvation are almost incalculable. The summary of these benefits appears in words true of every believer: *complete in him*. What must never be forgotten is that this sublime declaration does *not* denote the privilege of a select few spiritual saints, but "all who are united to Christ."[9]

2. *Completeness in Christ by virtue of the baptism of the Spirit does away with the claims of second-blessing theology and Pentecostalism.*

It is as if the Colossian letter was purposely written in anticipation of the confusion that prevails in these last days in the church on the question of the fullness of spiritual blessing. The question is, does spiritual fullness reside in Christ and the salvation He brings, or does it occur as an experience of the Holy Spirit in a so-called baptism of the Spirit?

To this contemporary question, the epistle to the Colossians gives a clear and authoritative answer. According to its doctrinal emphasis, spiritual fullness for all believers is located in *no other place than in Jesus Christ*. In one of the most sublime Christological passages of the New Testament, Paul sets forth the deity, creatorship, and headship of Christ over the church (Col 1:15-19) and His absolute preeminence over all in His work of reconciliation (1:20-23). Therefore "in him *all* the fullness was pleased to dwell" (1:19, translated from the Greek).

The Colossian believers, like their modern second-blessing and Pentecostal brothers, were being tempted to look for fullness in something or someone *beyond* Christ. Modern Pentecostalism, for example, seeks the so-called baptism, called also the filling, by seeking the Holy Spirit Himself. This is a very serious matter. As Beasley-Murray aptly declares: "However indignantly [Pentecostals] would repudiate the charge, their separation between the church's experience of Christ and the work of the Holy Spirit entails them in the gravest heresy, and it should not for a moment be countenanced by the churches."[10]

The New Testament locates both the baptism of the Spirit and the filling of the Spirit in Christ (i.e., in salvation), not in something in addition to Christ. Christians can be filled and refilled with the Spirit because when they were saved and placed by the Spirit in Christ they were granted every spiritual blessing. This included the privilege of the continual filling as at the beginning (Ac 2:4; cf. Eph 1:3 with 5:18).

The filling of the Spirit, in other words, is possible because of the believer's position in Christ. As the Christian believes he is what he is in Christ, his position becomes his experience. He becomes filled with the Spirit by faith—not by works or fulfilling conditions. He enjoys spiritual fullness because his heritage in Christ is spiritual fullness. Nor does he need to seek fullness outside of what he is in Christ. He needs only to count on what he is in Christ to enjoy every spiritual blessing.

The apostle, in order to correct the error that was threatening the Colossians, focused their attention upon their objective, unchangeable position ("in Christ") rather than upon their subjective changeable state. Doggedly Paul declared to the Colossians, "You are *in Christ*. Therefore you possess fullness, because you are in Him in whom all fulness dwells."

To insist that the believer, though in Christ, still needs some additional sort of spiritual fulfillment or appropriation, was the Colossian heresy. Christ was apparently not denied at Colossae; His Person and finished redemption were simply, and doubtlessly unconsciously, slighted. The Colossian teachers very likely believed they were honoring Christ by seeking deeper experiences on conditions of self-abasement, legalistic regulations, self-emptying, asceticism, and false mysticism (Col 2:18-23).

Little did the Colossians realize that they had abandoned faith for human effort, and the all-sufficiency of Christ and His redemptive work for self-trust and self-preoccupation. Small wonder present-day saints who fall into the Colossian error become occupied with experiences (what they are in themselves) rather than with Christ (what they are in Him). The tendency in these circles is to doubt the security of the believer, to operate on experience rather than on sound doctrine, and to have little or no assurance of eternal salvation. No wonder those who do not realize or count on their position in Christ think they have a salvation they can lose, if they don't hold out. Martin Luther states:

> So it is final, says St. Paul, the whole, total Godhead dwells bodily, that is personally, in Jesus Christ. Therefore the fellow who does not find or get God in Christ shall never again and nowhere else have or find God outside of Christ, even if he goes, as it were, over heaven, under hell, or into space.[11]

3. *The baptism of the Holy Spirit effects spiritual circumcision.*

With regard to his position in Christ the believer is not only complete in Him, he is also circumcised in Him. "In whom also ye are circumcised" (Col 2:11). In each case the benefit mentioned is the result of the believer's union and identification with Christ by the Spirit's baptism, including coburial and coresurrection, as in Romans 6:3-4. "Buried with him in baptism, wherein ye also are risen with him" (Col 2:12).

But what is this circumcision with which the believer is said to be circumcised? It is declared to be "circumcision made without hands," that is, a spiritual reality and not a physical rite, the antitype and not the type. Physical circumcision involved putting off part of the flesh as a symbol of covenant relationship between God and His people. Christian circumcision is a "putting off," not of a part, but of the entire "body of the flesh."[12]

The body of the flesh is the physical body controlled by the old fallen nature, which all possess, saved as well as unsaved. Putting off means stripping off, as one has discarded an old garment. It is positional truth, like the crucifixion of the old man in Romans 6:6 and being "dead indeed unto sin" and "alive unto God" in Romans 6:11. These expressions portray how God sees us in Christ.

Because the sin nature was judged by Christ in His death, so the believer shares that putting off which Christ accomplished, just as he shares His fullness and is declared to be complete in Him.

The believer's circumcision is not only a spiritual reality consisting in putting off the body of the flesh, it is more precisely Christ's circumcision, accomplished by Him and imputed to the believer: "In whom also ye are circumcised . . . by the *circumcision of Christ*" (Col 2:11).

Our Lord's circumcision mentioned in this passage does not refer to His physical circumcision when He was eight days old. It is rather a meaningful term the apostle applies to Christ's death to the sin nature.[13] It is the truth enunciated in Romans 6:10. "For in that he died, he died unto sin once," and Romans 8:3-4, "For what the law could not do, in that it was weak through the flesh, God sending his own Son in the likeness of sinful flesh, and for sin, condemned sin in the flesh, that the righteousness of the law might be fulfilled in us, who walk not after the flesh, but after the Spirit."

The believer stands before God as one whose sin nature has been divinely judged. In behalf of him God can righteously undertake in furnishing a way of deliverance from the dominion of the flesh. This is a position which grace has provided every believer and the baptism of the Spirit has consummated on the basis of a finished redemption.[14]

4. *The baptism of the Holy Spirit is the basis of a heavenly walk.*

The truth of union and identification with Christ in Colossians is employed by Paul to plead for a heavenly walk as he uses it in Romans 6 to provide for a holy walk. In Colossians the Christian's position in Christ is set forth as one in which Christ is the believer's life (3:4). The believer died with Christ (3:3), was buried with Christ (2:12), was raised with Him (3:1), and by implication is installed with Him at the right hand of God (3:1), one day to be glorified with Him (3:4).

Paul stresses a wonderful aspect of the Spirit's baptizing ministry, which makes possible a holy life here and now in a sinful world and in an unglorified body possessing an old nature. This is identification with Christ in burial. The believer is buried with Christ in baptism.

"The body of the sins of the flesh" has not only been put to death and judged before the mind and reckoning of God, but actually buried with Christ. The result is that the believer *now* on earth can live a heavenly life because he is raised with Christ and has the spiritual power available in being associated with Christ, His life (see also Gal 2:20).

All this accomplished by Spirit baptism is reflected outwardly and symbolically by water baptism, which "proclaims that the old order is over and done with . . . that a new order has been inaugurated."[15]

Using the exalted position of the believer in Christ, identified with Him in death, burial, resurrection, exaltation and life, as the ground of his plea, Paul urges that Christ shall become the believer's life *now*. The believer is to seek heavenly and not earthly things. This will result in a heavenly walk, which will be conformable to his heavenly position in Christ.

The Baptism of the Holy Spirit in First Peter 3:21

The revelation of the church as the body of Christ formed by the baptizing work of the Holy Spirit was given to the apostle Paul. In his epistles we find the full doctrinal exposition of the far-reaching ramifications of the truth which was unrevealed in the Old Testament, prophetic in the gospels, and historic in the Acts. The apostle Peter, however, makes a passing reference to Spirit baptism, which, although quite illuminating, adds nothing new to the Pauline doctrine.

This passage, is, on the other hand, an exceedingly important reference because it has been applied widely to water baptism, thus furnishing encouragement to error and false ritualism.

Peter shows what Paul all along has been showing, that water baptism is always implicit in Spirit baptism. But Peter stresses the vital truth that the implicit (water baptism) must never be substituted for the explicit (Spirit baptism).

1. *The baptizing work of the Holy Spirit is in view in 1 Peter 3:21*.

That the baptism to which Peter makes reference is in reality Spirit baptism is proved by several clear-cut facts.

First, only the baptizing work of the Holy Spirit can save. The unanimous testimony of Scripture is that no external rite can place one in Christ. Therefore Peter must be refering to the Spirit's baptizing work when he declares, "baptism doth also now save us." The apostle can only be thinking of the baptism of the Spirit as a present benefit of Christ's finished work of salvation.

A second observation indicating Peter's reference is to Spirit baptizing is that water baptism only saves figuratively, not actually. He limits the baptism which "doth now save us" to the reality, not the shadow, by a qualifying phrase. "Baptism doth now save us." How? "In a similar figure," that is, in a corresponding likeness. He illustrates his point by employing the typology of the flood.

How were "the few, that is, eight souls" of the antediluvian generation saved? He answers, "by water." This water cut them off from the sinners of that day, who were under divine judgment. So we are saved "by spiritual baptism," which removes us from the sphere of sin and condemnation.[16] But this is only negative. The eight antediluvians would have perished in the water rather than be saved by the water. They were saved by entering the ark: "While the ark was a preparing wherein few, that is, eight souls were saved by water." The believer is saved by Spirit baptism, not because he is merely negatively cut off from a state of sin and judgment, but positively by being placed in the antitypical ark, Christ, by the Spirit's baptism. Likewise the Israelites later were saved from Egypt (the world) and Pharaoh (Satan) by the waters of the Red Sea, being "baptized unto [into] Moses [Christ] in the cloud and in the sea" (1 Co 10:2).

A third observation indicating Peter's reference is to Spirit baptism is his own emphatic declaration in the context that *no mere external rite can actually save.* So careful is he that his readers might not misunderstand him, that he goes to great length to show that no outward ordinance is meant. This he does by a detailed negative qualifying definition, "not the putting away of the filth of the flesh" (v. 21). Then he adds a positive statement: "But the answer of a good conscience toward God."

The negative qualification shows that the apostle means nothing external or superficial in his use of the term *baptism*. The positive qualification, on the other hand, demonstrates clearly that he has in mind something internal and vital, spiritual and soul-transforming, which alone can be postulated for that glorious transaction which puts the believer in Christ and into His body.

The apostle Peter gives a final proof that the baptism he speaks of is Spirit baptism by connecting it directly with the resurrection. "The like figure whereunto even baptism doth also now save us . . . by the resurrection of Jesus Christ" (1 Pe 3:21). The intervening words between the "baptism doth also now save" and "by the resurrection of Jesus Christ" are but a parenthesis. The apostle establishes the direct connection between the baptism he has in mind (not ritual baptism) and the resurrection of Christ.[17]

This declaration of Peter so closely connecting Spirit baptism and Christ's resurrection emphasizes the illuminating fact that there was not, nor indeed could there be, any baptism by the Spirit into Christ's body until after Christ's resurrection. The death, burial, resurrection, and ascension of our Lord (v. 22) were all necessary steps to the giving of the Spirit at Pentecost to perform His unique baptizing ministry during this age. Without the resurrection all collapses. The resurrection gives us an everliving, life-giving Lord, the head of the new creation (2 Co 5:17). The Spirit's baptizing work puts us in Him (Ro 6:3, 4), and in the new creation in Him (Eph 1:20-23), and in all that He is (Col 2:10).

This ministry is the foundation of all our positions and possessions in Christ. It identifies us in death, burial, and resurrection with our glorified Lord (Ro 6:3-5) and unites us to Him in His ascension and present session (Eph 2:6) as well as His glorious coming again (Col 3:4). In fact, it makes us one for time and eternity with the most wonderful person in the universe, Jesus Christ our Lord.

8

The Baptism of the Spirit and the Gifts of the Spirit

MISUNDERSTANDING the baptism of the Spirit invariably leads to misunderstanding the gifts of the Spirit. The Pentecostal interpretation of the baptism of the Spirit as an experience subsequent to conversion distorts the true biblical perspective of the gifts of the Spirit. It is precisely for this reason the apostle Paul presents the correct doctrine of Spirit baptism (1 Co 12:12-13) in his great passage on the gifts of the Spirit in 1 Corinthians 12-14.

The apostle presents the baptism of the Spirit as a vital part of salvation and not an experience subsequent to salvation. "For by one Spirit we were all baptized into one body . . . and we were all made to drink of one Spirit" (1 Co 12:13, NASB). Moreover, he reveals that this baptism is both the basis of the unity of *all* believers in the body and the ground of the exercise of spiritual gifts in the body (1 Co 12:14-31).

SPIRITUAL GIFTS AND THE CLAIMS OF CHARISMATIC CHRISTIANITY

1. *Pentecostals contend that the baptism of the Spirit qualifies for the gifts of the Spirit.*

It is commonly believed among Pentecostals and Neo-Pentecostals that the believer is not endowed with his particular gift or gifts of the Spirit till he is baptized in the Spirit. Only at his baptism in the Spirit (which he views as a second experience), or sometime after this experience, does the believer become eligible for the full equipment of the spiritual gifts.

This contention is true under a correct definition of Spirit baptism as a vital part of salvation. But it cannot possibly be true under the erroneous notion of Spirit baptism as an experience later than salvation. A true deduction cannot be made from a false premise. Charismatic confusion concerning Spirit baptism is in large part the reason for charismatic confusion concerning spiritual gifts.

Pentecostals not only equate the baptism of the Spirit with an experience after salvation but also identify it with the gift of the Spirit. They then proceed to differentiate between the gift and the gifts.[1] The gift, under their interpretation, represents the experience in the book of Acts, namely the baptism of the Spirit with the initial glossolalic evidence. The gifts, on the other hand, represent the experience of the book of 1 Corinthians, especially 12:8-10.

They allege that the gift (the baptism) occurs only once, while the gifts are intended to be experienced continually. But the important point of Pentecostal belief is that gifts cannot exist at all—or at least cannot be manifested fully—until one receives the gift of the Holy Spirit. Their conclusion, then, is that a believer cannot have gifts of the Spirit until he has been baptized *in* the Holy Spirit with the initial evidence of tongues.

Further, they suggest this experience of tongues-evidenced baptism means the personal, permanent, and full entry of the Holy Spirit into the believer's life, qualifying him for the complete equipment of the spiritual gifts. The gift (the Pentecostal-tongues baptism) is assigned the general purpose of enduing the recipient with "power for service," while the gifts of the Spirit endow the Spirit-baptized, empowered believer with "a spiritual capacity far mightier than the finest natural abilities could ever supply."[2]

It has been noted in preceding chapters that the Pentecostal concept of "the gift of the Spirit" as the baptism of the Spirit is unwarranted from Scripture. The gift of the Spirit in reality is the initial once-for-all giving of the Holy Spirit by the ascended Christ (Jn 14:16-17) to work out the free gift of salvation in Jew (Ac 1:5; 2:38-39), in racially mongrel Samaritan (Ac 8:14-16) and in Gentile (Ac 10:45).

The term *gift of the Spirit,* therefore, does *not* refer to some experience subsequent to salvation but to salvation itself. Nor does the phrase refer to a gift to be received today. It was received over nineteen centuries ago at Pentecost and has been the permanent deposit of the church ever since and the heritage of each believer the moment he trusts Christ and experiences salvation.

Pentecost witnessed the reception of the gift of the Holy Spirit (Ac 2:38). "In that one gift of the Spirit, the ascension present of our Lord to His church, was included all the Spirit's ministries as well as His gifts, graces and power—his ministry of regenerating, baptizing, sealing, anointing and filling."[3]

How can the baptism of the Spirit be a second experience when it is an integral part of the gift of the Spirit and hence inseparable from salvation? In reality *all* saved people are a deposit of the gift of the Spirit, are baptized by the Spirit into Christ, and are recipients of the varied gifts of the Spirit for service in the church, the body of Christ. Hence, the baptism of the Spirit does qualify for the gifts of the Spirit, but emphatically not as something additional to salvation, as Pentecostals claim, but as a vital part of salvation itself.

2. *Pentecostals claim that all the gifts manifested in the early church ought to be in operation in the church today.*

This is a logical deduction from the doctrine of the baptism of the Spirit as a second experience evidenced by tongues-speaking. Pentecostals and Neo-Pentecostals lay special emphasis upon the list of nine gifts enumerated by the apostle Paul in 1 Corinthians 12:8-10. They contend that all of these nine gifts, including the miraculous sign gifts, are still in the church today and should be exercised when God's people assemble for worship and fellowship.

The church in general has always maintained, on the basis of Scripture and the testimony of history, that the so-called miraculous sign gifts of healing and tongues, gradually disappeared from the church after the apostolic age when the New Testament was written down and circulated among the churches. Pentecostals, however, deny that any of the gifts were temporary and hence suspended.

The Pentecostal holds that the gifts were never withdrawn by God but were lost as a result of the worldliness and unbelief of the church.[4] Pentecostals like to think that in their movement God is demonstrating what He can do with a church that believes in and exercises all the gifts of the Spirit.

Neo-Pentecostal Christians, in agreement with older Pentecostal believers, hold to the permanence of the apostolic gifts and insist that all of them should be in operation in the church today. Laurence Christenson asserts, "when the body of Christ is functioning in a normal way—normal by New Testament standards—the gifts of the Spirit which Paul lists in 1 Corinthians 12 will come into manifestation . . . as they are needed."[5] Kevin and Dorothy Ranaghan declare: "The shattering difference [the Neo-Pentecostal movement has wrought] is an unexpected return to the primitive list of ministry gifts as mentioned in First Corinthians 12:8-10.[6]

To bolster its position concerning the gifts of the Spirit Pentecostalism marshalls Romans 11:29: "the gifts and the calling of God are irrevocable" (Ro 11:29, NASB), "Jesus is the same yesterday and today, yes and forever" (Heb 13:8, NASB), and the textually questionable passage of Mark 16:17-20.

In addition to Scripture, Pentecostals appeal to human need to support their doctrine of spiritual gifts. They maintain the need for these gifts is just as great, if not greater, today than in the apostolic church. "Has [God] happened upon a period of temporary helplessness in this age of desperate human need?" asks Horton.[7]

The Pentecostal is persuaded that Scripture authenticates the gifts and human need necessitates them. He further believes the baptism of the Spirit is the source of the church's power and the gifts of the Spirit the medium of this power.

SPIRITUAL GIFTS AND THE WITNESS OF THE WORD

1. *Spiritual gifts are the endowment of all members of the body of Christ.*

Scripture reveals that *all* believers are in the body of Christ by virtue of Spirit baptism, and that *all* possess one or more gifts of the Spirit as a result. This, as already noted, is the clear declaration of the central passage on the baptism of the Spirit, 1 Co 12:13.* This basic truth, denied by Pentecostal teaching, is featured in the first of the three chapters the apostle devotes to the doctrine of spiritual gifts, 1 Corinthians 12, and particularly in verses 12-26.

In this great passage several cardinal doctrines are set forth, all generally at variance with Pentecostal teaching. First, *the body of Christ is one.* It is not two bodies—one of ordinary believers, the other of Spirit-baptized believers. "For even as the body is one" (1 Co 12:12).

Second, *the basis of the unity of the one body is the believer's position in Christ.* This unity centers in his being baptized into Christ, not allegedly his being baptized (immersed) in the Holy Spirit. The one body, declares the apostle, "has many members, and all the members of the body, though they are many, are one body, so also is Christ" (1 Co 12:12, NASB). By the highly significant comparison the apostle is not referring to the literal Christ, the resurrected, glorified Lord at the right hand of the Father. He is clearly designating the mystical Christ. He specifically means the triumphant Christ in heaven joined to His people—the church, His body on earth.

Third, *the believer's position in Christ is secured by the Spirit's work in baptism.* Christ and His body, the church, are united by the baptism of the Spirit. "For by one Spirit we were all baptized into one body, whether Jews or Greeks, whether slaves or free" (1 Co 12:13, NASB). This is Spirit baptism whether the Greek preposition *en* is construed as the instrumental *by* or the locative of sphere *in*. To show the precise meaning in Greek of the phrase *Spirit baptism,* we can express it in English as in-the-sphere-of-the-Spirit baptism. Baptism in

*See introduction to this chapter.

water, the ritual, is only a sign or symbol, and meaningless apart from the spiritual reality (see also Mt 3:11; Mk 1:8; Lk 3:16-17; Jn 1:33; Ac 1:5; 2:38; 8:16, 35-38; 10:47-48; 19:4-5).

Fourth, *the believer's position in Christ is the ground of His experience of His position.* *All* believers were baptized by or in the sphere of the Spirit the moment they were saved. Their resultant position in Christ enables them to enjoy a Spirit-filled experience of Christ. They "were *all* made to drink of one Spirit" (1 Co 12:13b). Spirit baptism, accordingly, transfers the sinner who trusts Christ's redemptive work from the desert where he is dying of thirst and places him before a fountain of water, even putting a cup in his hand, so that he may drink again and again from an inexhaustible supply (see Jn 7:37-39).

Fifth, *the body of Christ, the church, is the sphere in which the gifts of the Spirit are exercised.* The variously gifted members of the body are compared to various organs of the human body. As each member of the human body has its function and place in the body, fulfilling a definite need, so each member of Christ's mystical body, the church, has his gift which he is to minister in the body and for the health and efficient operation of the body as a whole (1 Co 12:14-26).

2. *Spiritual gifts in the apostolic church included the temporary, miraculous sign-gifts.*

The earliest list of gifts, nine in number, include at least four that were miraculous and employed in part at least, as sign gifts—gifts of healing, the working of miracles, tongues, and interpretation of tongues (1 Co 12:8-10). The believers at Corinth were richly endowed with spiritual gifts, including the miraculous ones, so that Paul could say they were not lacking in any gift (1 Co 1:7).

Such miraculous sign-gifts were the special endowment of the apostles, as the God-ordained founders of Christianity. To the Corinthians Paul declared, "The signs of a true apostle were performed among you with all perseverance, by signs and wonders and miracles" (2 Co 12:12, NASB). These supernatural gifts, which he exercised and was able to transmit to others, served not only to establish Christianity but to vindicate his apostleship. Paul performed the same kind of signs and wonders on his first missionary tour for the same reasons (Ac 14:3). In the Roman letter too, Paul refers to what Christ accomplished through him "in the power of signs and wonders in the power of the Spirit" in his ministry among the pagan nations (Ro 15:18-19, NASB).

The writer to the Hebrews mentions the purpose of the miraculous sign gifts. He intimates it was to confirm the gospel and establish the new faith in a pagan world. "How shall we escape if we neglect so great a salvation? After it was at the first spoken through the Lord, it was confirmed to us by those who heard, God also bearing witness with them, both by signs and wonders and by various miracles and by gifts of the Holy Spirit according to His own will" (Heb 2:3-4, NASB).

This passage clearly refers to the ministry of the Lord and the apostles who heard Him. "The gifts [distributions] of the Holy Spirit" embrace such charismata as are enumerated in 1 Corinthians 12:8-10.

But as credentials of an apostle and as confirmation of the gospel, these miraculous charismata passed away after the apostolic period, when apostles no longer existed and the Christian faith no longer needed such outward signs to confirm it. This important fact is not only intimated by Scripture but well attested by church history.[8]

This does not mean that God upon occasion may not, for His highest glory and to meet a human need, grant special faith to some or the power to perform miracles, including miracles of healing, or endow a missionary with the ability to preach to a tribe in a language he never learned, if circumstances so necessitate. These divine manifestations, however, are not to be regarded as gifts, but simply as individual acts of God.

A gift implies a settled and continued ability to do something again and again. While God, of course, can do miracles and certainly performs them today, He does not dispense the gift of miracles as in the early church. To establish and authenticate the new faith, apostles and miracle workers were needed and

abounded. Now that the faith has been established, no such
need exists and no such gifts abound. Faith is to rest in a completed, written revelation, authenticated by miracle and fulfilled prophecy. Now we are to "walk by faith, not by sight"
(2 Co 5:7).

It is true, "Jesus Christ is the same yesterday and today, yes
and forever" (Heb 13:8, NASB). But it is emphatically not
true that the need for signs and miracles to attend the ministry
of the Word is the same now as it was in the early church. Then
the gift of an apostle was given, because needed (1 Co 12:28).
It is obvious this gift was temporary. Could this not suggest
that other spiritual gifts may also have been temporary?

3. *Spiritual gifts in the apostolic church also included the temporary revelatory gifts.*

These are the special gifts of the Spirit manifest in the early
church enabling first-century assemblies to meet and have a
preaching-teaching service before the New Testament was
written and circulated among the churches. These revelatory
gifts are included in the earliest list presented in 1 Corinthians
12:8-10 and form the subject of the passage 13:8-13.

The revelatory gifts contained in the list in 1 Corinthians
12:8-10 are the word of knowledge, prophecy, various kinds
of tongues. In 1 Corinthians 13:8, the order is prophecies,
tongues, knowledge.

The very first fact to perceive about the apostle's teaching
in 1 Corinthians 13 is that he is talking about *gifts*—the gift
of prophecy issuing in prophecies and the gift of knowledge.
The apostle emphatically does not have in mind the ability
through study of the prophetic Word to propound biblical
prophecy. He means specifically an endowment of the Holy
Spirit enabling a first-century believer, through extrabiblical
revelation of the future, to declare truth now enshrined in the
prophecies of the New Testament.

Nor does Paul have in mind knowledge of the written Word,
much less knowledge in a general sense. He refers *strictly* to
the *gift* of knowledge. By this special gift the Holy Spirit en-

abled a first-century believer to know and to instruct the assembly in truth now recorded in the New Testament.

It must be remembered that 1 Corinthians is one of the earlier epistles, written in all probability before A.D. 57. When it was penned there was practically no New Testament in existence, except the epistle of James addressed to Hebrew Christians and 1 and 2 Thessalonians. But there were no New Testament manuscripts to preach from. The Old Testament, of course, was available for study, but it did not cover the great distinctive teachings of the new age.

The question may be asked, could the Corinthian assembly meet and have a teaching ministry? The answer is yes. God graciously endowed the early church with special revelatory gifts of prophecy, tongues (when interpreted), and knowledge. These special temporary gifts met an urgent need. They were designed to tide the church through the period of partial, piecemeal revelation until the complete and final thing would arrive (1 Co 13:10).

The apostle describes that early period of partial, piecemeal revelation in the words: "For we know in part and we prophecy in part" (1 Co 13:9). He is *not* speaking of today but of his day, before the New Testament became available for study and exposition. Then a believer endowed with the gift of prophecy stood up in the meeting in A.D. 57 and by direct revelation from the Spirit taught on the rapture or the judgment seat of Christ or the marriage of the Lamb or the New Jerusalem. But all this teaching was bit by bit and fragmentary. Another would rise and discourse in a language he had never studied. He would speak mysteries, and another would interpret to the congregation. So the end result would be equivalent to the gift of prophecy or knowledge.

Another with the gift of knowledge would stand to his feet and discourse on the church, the body of Christ, or the gifts of the Spirit, or the believer's position in Christ, etc. But again this ministry was partial and piecemeal. Here a little, there a little, in contrast to "the perfect [complete] thing" (1 Co 13:10). This passage, by strict adherence to the context, necessitates interpreting the complete thing as the New Testament Scriptures, added to the Old Testament and constituting the completed, written revelation of God, forming the canonical Scripture.

Those who study God's Word do not know partially or prophesy partially. The completeness and finality of the Word gives completeness and finality to the teaching of those who faithfully expound it.

For this very reason the apostle tells exactly why the three revelatory gifts in contrast to everenduring love (1 Co 13:1-8) were not meant to be permanent throughout the age. Two of them—the gift of prophecies and the gift of knowledge—were to be rendered useless and unnecessary by something better, and so be done away with, just like the old horse and buggy of the nineteenth century have been cancelled out by the automobile of the twentieth century.

The gift of tongues,† like the gift of prophecy and the gift of knowledge, belongs to a period of partial revelation before there were any New Testament books in circulation. Probably because of the very limited use of tongues, even in the early church, except an interpreter was present, they are said to cease, literally "stop of themselves" (middle voice).

History bears out the Scripture teaching. Tongues faded out and were silent among the evangelical people of God for nineteen hundred years, even in holiness and second-blessing circles until the rise of the twentieth-century tongues-speaking phenomenon.

It is, however, a strange anomaly that Pentecostals and Neo-Pentecostals champion the gift of tongues for today, yet inconsistently reject extrabiblical prophecies and extrabiblical knowledge by special gifts of the Holy Spirit. Pentecostals, like non-Pentecostals, study the Word and make it the source of their spiritual knowledge and prophetic instruction. They do not rely upon the pronouncements of believers who claim the gift of prophecy or the gift of knowledge today apart from the written Word.

---

†Tongues-speaking fits in the category of both a sign gift and a revelatory gift.

4. *The apostle's great doctrinal passage on the gifts of the Spirit supplies the cure for present-day charismatic confusion.*

The twelfth chapter of 1 Corinthians furnishes the correct doctrine of Spirit baptism, showing it to be a vital part of our salvation, true of *all* believers, and the ground of the exercise of their gifts in the body of Christ (1 Co 12:12-26). Not at all is it a second experience after salvation, much less evidenced by tongues (1 Co 12:30). Attempts to deduce a Pentecostal baptism distinct from the one spiritual baptism of 1 Corinthians 12:13 (see also Eph 4:5) are doomed to failure if sound Bible exposition is followed.

The thirteenth chapter of 1 Corinthians answers the controversial question of the permanence of the gifts. In fact, the question of the permanency of certain gifts is *the* subject of the chapter, not, as popularly supposed, the topic of love. It is perhaps the love chapter, but only incidentally. Love is introduced *contextually* only to contrast its permanency, as the queen of all the virtues, with the impermanence of certain spiritual gifts, specifically the three revelatory gifts—prophecy, tongues, and knowledge. By implication, a fourth gift is under consideration, too. Interpretation of tongues is always inseparably connected with tongues as a revelatory gift. Without interpretation, tongues were useless in the public assembly (see 1 Co 14:5, 19, 27).

The fourteenth chapter of 1 Corinthians regulates the manifestation of *all* nine of the gifts (1 Co 12:8-10) in the early church, where they were legitimate and, in fact, very much needed. This chapter *does not* regulate a condition that may and (from the Pentecostal and Neo-Pentecostal standpoint) *ought* to exist today.

If such were the case, the apostle would flatly contradict in this chapter what he has plainly declared concerning the revelatory gifts in the thirteenth chapter, that the gifts of prophecy, tongues, and knowledge would no longer be needed and no longer be manifested when the finished written revelation of God had arrived. Also, today's charismatic meetings ought to have in operation the revelatory gifts of prophecy and knowledge. This would mean extrabiblical revelations, like those of Emanuel Swedenborg, the founder of Swedenborgianism, and Joseph Smith, the apostle of Mormonism.

But our Pentecostal and neo-Pentecostal friends have always professed loyalty to the Word of God and faithfully, if inconsistently in this case, have regarded it as the sole source of inspired truth, complete in its revelation, and needing no gifts furnishing extrabiblical revelations.

One of the arguments charismatic believers use for championing a revival of all the spiritual gifts of the early church is that urgent needs in these times make these gifts necessary. But this argument fails because the twentieth-century church has what the apostolic church did not have, namely, the completed canon of fully inspired and authoritative Scripture. This priceless treasure has superseded the revelatory gifts, making them unnecessary.

In addition, the twentieth-century church has an established gospel and a faith that has proved its power to save for over nineteen centuries. This faith, unlike the young faith of the first century, has been fully authenticated by apostolic, miraculous sign gifts and by the test of time. It needs no such authentication today. Those who believe the gospel and embrace the great salvation it offers are to "walk by faith, not by sight" (2 Co 5:7).

5. *Will the Bible or experience be the decisive criterion for Christians in the seventies?*

The apostle Paul, in his teaching on the impermanence of the revelatory gifts in the light of the completed, written revelation of God (1 Co 13:8-10), furnishes the inspired guidelines for believers in these days of confusion.

Theodore Epp, director of the Back to the Bible Broadcast of Lincoln, Nebraska, issues a timely warning:

> Because experience is emphasized above the teaching of the Bible, many in this [charismatic] movement do not believe that there is a closed, historical, supernatural revelation from God. They do not believe that God's revelation of truth ceased when He gave us the whole Bible. They continue to

accept certain revelations as inspired truth from God, whether it is through visions, dreams, or messages received by hearing some kind of voices.

There are those who even go so far as to say that the Bible tells about Christ, but the experience is Christ Himself speaking. If those who say this really know what they are saying, it is blasphemy. The Bible makes it clear that not only does Jesus speak through the Bible, but also His words are life (John 6:63).

Apart from the Bible we have no revelation of Jesus Christ. We shall never know more of Him, in this life, than we know from the Bible. We grow in our understanding of Christ, but we do not receive more information about Christ.[9]

9

The Baptism of the Holy Spirit and Power

TODAY IN MANY CHRISTIAN CIRCLES, charismatic as well as noncharismatic, the baptism of the Spirit is generally connected with the power of the Spirit for holy living and effective service. Anyone who undertakes to define precisely the biblical relation between the two truths risks being accused of trying to rob the individual Christian of blessing and the church of its dynamic for soul-winning zeal and revival fire.[1] But whatever misunderstanding the careful Bible student might face, he must, nevertheless, clearly set forth the plain distinctions of the Word on this matter. Rather than robbing any Christian of blessing or the church of its dynamic for soul-winning and revival, these teachings will minister to every spiritual benefit and advance.

The correct scriptural doctrine of the Holy Spirit has always been a factor for strength and the basis of the church's progress. The present appalling condition of God's people—with the invasion of unbelief and worldliness on one hand and the rise of numerous sects and cults on the other—can be diagnosed in the light of the doctrine of the baptizing work of the Spirit. This state of affairs is due to ignorance and neglect of this truth in the one instance and misconception and misguided zeal regarding it on the other. The correct Biblical teaching on the Spirit's baptizing work always ministers to the unity, purity, and power of the church of Christ.

THE BAPTISM OF THE HOLY SPIRIT THE BASIS OF POWER

1. *The believer's position in Christ is the ground for his appropriation of power.* Since the Christian is placed in the body of

147

Christ (1 Co 12:13) and into Christ Himself by the Spirit's baptizing work (Ro 6:3, 4; Gal 3:27), and since all his spiritual possessions (including power for holy living and effective serving) spring out of that position, the baptism with the Spirit is the basis of the appropriation of power. However, it in itself is *not* the reception of power. To confuse the basis of power with the appropriation of power clouds the understanding of the believer's position in Christ and exposes the appropriation of the power to error and fanaticism.

The epistle to the Ephesians constitutes an exposition of the believer's standing in union with Jesus Christ by the Spirit's baptizing work. The believer is blessed "with all spiritual blessings in heavenly places in Christ" (1:3), "accepted in the beloved" (1:6), in whom he also has "obtained an inheritance" (1:11), and in whom he was "sealed with that Holy Spirit of promise" (1:13). The apostle's fervent prayer was that God's people might understand this glorious position of union with Christ and *appropriate the power of that position.*

> Wherefore I also, after I heard of your faith in the Lord Jesus, and love unto all the saints, cease not to give thanks for you, making mention of you in my prayers; that the God of our Lord Jesus Christ, the Father of glory, may give unto you the spirit of wisdom and revelation in the knowledge of him: The eyes of your understanding being enlightened; that ye may know what is the hope of his calling, and what the riches of the glory of his inheritance in the saints, and what is *the exceeding greatness of his power to us-ward who believe, according to the working of his mighty power, which he wrought in Christ, when he raised him from the dead,* and set him at his own right hand in the heavenly places, far above all principality, and power, and might, and dominion, and every name that is named, not only in this world, but also in that which is to come: and hath put all things under his feet, and gave him to be head over all things to the church, which is his body, the fulness of him that filleth all in all (Eph 1:15-23).

As a member of the body of Christ, the believer is quickened with Him (2:5), raised up with Him, made to sit in heavenly places in Christ Jesus (2:6), in Christ Jesus brought close to God (2:13), and in union with Christ made a temple for the habitation of God through the Spirit (2:19-22), according to the revelation of the church as a mystery hidden from past ages (3:1-12). Again the apostle interrupts his exposition of the believer's position in Christ by the Spirit's baptizing work with another prayer, like the first, that God's people might understand this position of oneness with Christ and claim the *power* of it.

> For this cause I bow my knees unto the Father of our Lord Jesus Christ, of whom the whole family in heaven and earth is named, that he would grant you, according to the riches of his glory, *to be strengthened with might by his Spirit* in the inner man; that Christ may dwell in your hearts by faith; that ye, being rooted and grounded in love, may be able to comprehend with all saints what is the breadth, and length, and depth, and height; and to know the love of Christ, which passeth knowledge, that *ye might be filled with all the fulness of God.* Now unto him that is able to do exceeding abundantly above all that we ask or think, *according to the power that worketh in us,* unto him be glory in the church by Christ Jesus throughout all ages, world without end. Amen (Eph 3:14-21).

Ending the doctrinal section with a prayer and doxology in his exposition of the believer's exalted standing in heaven in Christ, the apostle passes on to the practical section of Ephesians (chapters 4-6), setting forth the believer's walk on earth as worthy of this position in the heavenlies in union with Christ. In the one baptism (4:5) he significantly refers to the momentous operation of the Spirit which is the basis of the believer's high position in Christ.

Before the practical section closes, the believer's walk merges into a warfare (Eph 6:10-20). In describing the Christian warrior's strength, the apostle makes a final reference which connects power for Christian conduct and conflict with the result of the Spirit's work baptizing the believer into Christ. "Finally, my brethren, *be strong* in the Lord and in the *power* of his *might*" (Eph 6:10).

The apostle is not emphasizing strength *from* the Lord, but first of all, *in* the Lord, the power that flows from the consciousness of union with the Lord. He would have us strong in the position which is ours in Him, just as the hand or foot has its strength in the body to which it belongs. The life union by the Spirit's baptizing work is the source of power. In Ephesians 6:10 three different words are required to describe the power which is available to every Christian by virtue of his oneness with his Lord: "Be *strong* in the Lord, and in the *power* of his *might*."

The phraseology is important. "Be strong *in the Lord*." In Ephesians the expression is almost uniformly "in Christ." The apostle in this case, however, does not use the official, mediatorial name, nor the personal, human name, Jesus. But significantly, he employs the divine name, Lord, of Him who is now our master (Jn 13:13) and the coming "King of kings and Lord of lords" (Rev 19:16). The thought is that the believer is to derive his strength from his oneness with Him who is his victorious Lord, who wrought victory for him in death, burial, resurrection, and ascension (Eph 1:15-23) and is coming to complete it in ultimate triumph. This is the fountainhead of the strength, might, and power which are the Christian's heritage, and there can be no substitute for it.

2. *The principle of appropriation of power is faith.* It is of the utmost importance for the believer to be acquainted with his position in Christ by the Spirit's baptizing work and to realize this union is the source of power. But knowledge, here as elsewhere in dealing with God's Word, is not sufficient. The Word preached and understood, in order to profit, must be "mixed with faith" in those who hear it (Heb 4:2). The believer's glorious position in Christ, at least as far as the experiential enjoyment of the power of it, will remain frozen assets of mere theological theory until the believer adds faith to his knowledge and converts the potentialities of his position into the practical experience of everyday living. As Charles Erdman says: "There is one condition of spiritual power; it con-

sists in maintaining a right relation to Christ: and this relation may be defined by the familiar term 'faith.' "[2]

"Why is faith so emphasized in Scripture? Because it is the only possible response to God's revelation. His faithfulness is to be met by my faith, His trust by my trust. He is trustworthy; therefore I must be trustful. Faith accepts all these things in Christ; faith claims them as a possession; faith appropriates them to personal use; faith uses them to the glory of God."[3]

The life of victory and joyous blessing, which the apostle enjoyed, he accordingly declared to be the result not merely of the knowledge of his position in Christ, but a hearty appropriation by faith of its benefits. "I have been crucified with Christ; and it is no longer I who live, but Christ lives in me; and the life which I now live in the flesh I live by faith in the Son of God, who loved me and delivered himself up for me" (Gal 2:20, NASB).

In Romans, receiving power for victory over sin in the matter of holy living is made not only contingent upon the believer's knowledge of his position of death, burial, and resurrection with Christ (Ro 6:1-10), but the reception of the benefits of that position by faith. "Likewise reckon ye also yourselves to be dead indeed unto sin, but alive unto God through [in union with] Jesus Christ our Lord" (Ro 6:11).

The word *reckon* is a word of faith. To reckon is to believe to be true what is true. What is true is that the believer *is* "dead indeed unto sin and alive unto God" by virtue of his position "in Jesus Christ our Lord." The fact of the believer's identification with his Lord resulting in a death-to-sin and an alive-to-God position remains true, to be sure, whether the Christian reckons or acts upon it in faith or not. The difference is that when he does act upon it in faith, the power of God is released in his experience and in his service.

That the believer's knowledge of his position in Christ is of incalculable importance is thus apparent. He cannot believe that of which he is totally ignorant or exercise an intelligent faith in that of which he may be only partially instructed. If there is to be a genuine faith to act upon his position in Christ to claim his possessions in Christ, there must be a clear apprehension of that position. It is upon the denial or faulty view of the believer's eternally secure and unforfeitable position in Christ that much of the unsound teaching on the baptism of the Holy Spirit is erected.

Since the believer's position in Christ is the basis of his appropriation of power on the ground of faith, to leave this solid scriptural foundation and to seek power on some other terms, is the explanation for much of the fanaticism, excesses, and abuses that attend the unscriptural use of the term *baptism of the Holy Spirit*.

The rise of a large-scale interdenominational charismatic movement since 1950, and the dawn of the age of the occult since 1970 with increased activity of demonic powers are sounding a new warning to believers against delusion and despoilment. The Word of God correctly interpreted and implicitly followed, especially in matters dealing with spiritual manifestations, is the only sure guarantee against Satanic imitation and demonic deception.

THE BIBLE TERMINOLOGY FOR POWER

1. *The baptism with the Holy Spirit is not a correct scriptural term for power.* Despite the widespread abuse of this term in the church of Christ in recent times, producing appalling confusion in doctrine and sad excesses in practice—warning enough of its essential unsoundness as a term for receiving power—many otherwise enlightened leaders and earnest soul-winners not only tenaciously refuse to abandon the inaccurate use of the expression, but earnestly defend the alleged scripturality of such usage and severely criticize those who insist upon strict biblical terminology, as if they were trying to deprive the church of its dynamic for holy living and witnessing.[4]

The fact remains, however, that those who insist on employing this term for power continually need to explain what they mean and what they think the Bible means by it. How much better it would be if they would employ the term as the Bible uses it. They would then unburden themselves of the need to rid it of the mistaken ideas which have become connected with it.

How does the Bible employ the terminology concerned? The much-used and much-abused term *baptism of the Holy Spirit* does not occur in Scripture, which speaks of being "baptized with the Spirit" (Mt 3:11), "baptized into one body" (1 Co 12:13), "baptized into Jesus Christ" (Ro 6:3-4; Gal 3:27), "one baptism" (Eph 4:5), but never "the baptism of the Holy Spirit." It is the Pentecostal contention that the baptism of the Spirit is meant to be a dramatic, critical *experience*—a veritable baptism *in* the Holy Spirit. This assumption forms the starting point of much present-day error on the subject.

The pivotal question is this: did not John the Baptist (Mt 3:11; Mk 1:8; Lk 3:16) and our Lord (Ac 1:5) distinctly refer to the mighty outpouring of the Holy Spirit at Pentecost (Ac 2:4) as the baptism with the Holy Spirit? The Word of God itself is the only valid witness to this question, foundational to the correct biblical doctrine of the Spirit's baptizing work. Regarding the power of Pentecost the divine word is not that "they were all baptized with the Holy Spirit," but "they were all filled with the Holy Spirit" (Ac 2:4).

But the filling of the Spirit was a peripheral, not a central manifestation at Pentecost. Central to the meaning of Pentecost was the giving, receiving, and permanent deposit of the gift of the Spirit and His coming and taking up of permanent residence (Jn 14:16; 16:12-13). Apart from the giving of the gift and the advent of the Spirit, there could not have been the filling. The filling was part of the gift and the advent was a prerequisite of the filling.

But what of the baptism of the Spirit? Like the filling, it too was part of the gift of the Spirit (Ac 1:5; 11:15-16). Prerequisite to it also was the giving of the gift of the Spirit and the advent of the Spirit.

However, this does not mean the baptism of the Spirit is the filling. The doctrinal epistles of the New Testament conclusively show that the baptism is the basis of the filling but not the filling itself. Both occurred at Pentecost. But the baptism was mentioned by our Lord not because it was the dramatic or experiential part of Pentecost, but because it was positional and nonexperiential, *basic not only to the filling, but to all the other ministries of the Spirit.*

Many teachers, however, have fallen into the subtle fallacy of making the filling with the Spirit in Acts 2:4 synonymous with the Spirit's baptizing ministry because John predicted that Messiah would baptize with the Holy Spirit and because our Lord Himself described the approaching advent of the Spirit at Pentecost in these words: "Ye shall be baptized with the Holy Spirit not many days hence" (Ac 1:5; cf. 11:14-16).[5]

But to identify the two ministries of the Spirit on this basis involves the assumption, not tenable in the light of the full New Testament teaching concerning the Spirit's baptizing work, that Pentecost was simply a matter of enduement with power. Pentecost was that, of course, and that is the feature that stands out in the manifestations of power and in the divine commentary of the event: "They were all filled with the Holy Spirit."

Pentecost, however, was much more than a mighty filling with the Holy Spirit to empower the infant church for witnessing and growth. This feature has been repeated in mighty outpourings throughout the church age; for example, at Herrnhut in Saxony upon the Moravian Brethren in 1727, in the Wesley and Whitefield revivals and the revival under Jonathan Edwards of the eighteenth century, in the revival under Charles G. Finney of the nineteenth century, and in so-called Pentecostal revivals of the twentieth century.

Most seekers after the power of Pentecost, on the other hand, have been oblivious to the fact that Pentecost was much more than an enduement with power. They forget that there are certain features of this event that are unique and cannot possibly be repeated. For example, Pentecost marked the advent of the Spirit. He came at that time and can never come again. He *is here.* He is therefore to be recognized as having arrived, no longer to be tarried for as the disciples waited for His coming from heaven in the upper room. Then, too, Pentecost witnessed the reception of the gift of the Holy Spirit (Ac 2:38).

It is to the age-inaugurating, unrepeatable features of Pentecost that the miraculous features of wind, fire, and tongues are to be attributed—namely, *to the giving of the gift of the Spirit and the advent of the Spirit, not* to the baptism of the Spirit or the filling of the Spirit.

In the *one* gift of the Spirit was included *all* of the Spirit's ministries as well as all His gifts, graces, and power—his ministry of regenerating, baptizing, sealing, anointing, and filling. It is precarious, then, to fasten upon just one of the varied ministries of the Spirit—the ministry of filling—and to assume that Jesus had reference only to that when He said, "ye shall be baptized with the Holy Spirit not many days hence" (Ac 1:5).

The unique features of Pentecost must be constantly kept in mind if this widely misunderstood event is not to continue to be a prolific source of unsound teaching and a spawning ground for new sects. Charismatic leaders build doctrines on the second chapter of Acts without once examining them in the light of the types and prophecies of the Old Testament or testing them in the crucible of the great doctrinal epistles of the New Testament.

The ancient Hebrew Feast of Weeks (Lev 23:15-21), as a type of what happened in Acts 2, clearly demonstrates the unique and never-to-be-repeated aspects of Pentecost. The Passover (Lev 23:4-5) sacrificed on the fourteenth day of the first month speaks of the death of Christ, and the Feast of First-fruits (Lev 23:9-14) on the morrow after the Sabbath three days later portrays the resurrection of Christ. Pentecost (Lev 23:15-21) fifty days later sets forth the coming of the Holy Spirit (Ac 2:1-4). It is obvious from the type that the Holy Spirit arrived in Acts 2 and is present in the church so that this feature of Pentecost can never be repeated. It is also evident the Spirit came not because the disciples prayed or tarried for Him (though they did both), but because it was the scheduled time for His arrival in the divine timetable (Ac 2:1). Abraham Kuyper well summarizes the revealed evidence. "Wherefore it cannot be doubted that the Holy Scripture means to teach and convince us that the outpouring of the Holy Spirit on Pentecost was His first real coming into the church."[6] How unscriptural, then, are prayers and hymns that are requests for the Spirit's advent, ignoring the fact that He has already come.

The Old Testament type, moreover, demonstrates other unique features of Pentecost. The Spirit not only arrived at the divinely scheduled time but came to take up, among His other ministries, His special baptizing work, which is confined to the present church age. The typical foreshadowing of Pentecost in Leviticus gives prominence to the results to be accomplished by this new and revolutionary ministry. Both John the Baptist and Jesus emphasized this feature of Pentecost in their predictions—John indicating that Messiah should baptize with the Holy Spirit (Jn 1:32, 33) and Jesus describing this as a prominent feature of Pentecost (Ac 1:5).

In the type, a new meat (meal) offering was to be presented to the Lord (Lev 23:16). The meal offering of Leviticus 2 portrays Christ, but the *new* meal offering speaks of something else. As H. K. Downie says: "What is it but the Church, which is the body and bride of Christ? The Church is a new revelation in the ways of God with men. There was nothing quite like it in the ages preceding Pentecost. We are explicitly informed that the secret regarding it was deliberately withheld and intentionally hidden from those who lived in other ages (Eph. 3:5)."[7]

The new meal offering at the Feast of Pentecost was called new because it was from the grain of the new harvest. At the Feast of First-fruits, typifying Christ risen, a sheaf of grain was offered and waved (Lev 23:11), but at Pentecost the grain was to be ground into flour, from which two loaves were to be baked. The union of many grains of wheat to form bread is a picture of the oneness of the church of Christ made by the Spirit's baptizing work at Pentecost. Although there are two loaves, prefiguring union of Jew and Gentile in the body of Christ (Eph 3:6), the bread is one. "For we being many are one bread, and one body" (1 Co 10:17).

The two loaves were of fine flour baked with leaven (Lev 23:17). The fine flour (Lev 2) speaks of Christ, who indwells every Christian, and the leaven points to the evil of the old nature, which also is present beside the new nature in the child of God, and is the source of evil and corruption in the church. But it must not be forgotten that the *leaven was baked*. It became inactive because it had passed through the fire, just as God's judgment was executed against the old nature in the flesh through the death of Christ (Ro 8:3), so that the Christian may have victory over it. Moreover, the ten animal sacrifices offered with the new meal offering in the ancient Feast (Lev 23:18-21) picture Christ, through whom the church is presented to God and fully accepted by virtue of His glorious Person. On the basis of His finished work, He baptized the disciples into one body through the Holy Spirit on the day of Pentecost.

In the light of Old Testament typology, the denial that the church began on the day of Pentecost and the contention that the term "baptized with the Holy Spirit" means physical manifestations and the power for soul-winning are unjustified. More serious than ignoring Old Testament typology is the failure to test thoroughly doctrines erected on the gospels and the Acts in the crucible of the great doctrinal epistles of the New Testament. Old-line Pentecostals and Neo-Pentecostals in the present-day charismatic movement base their doctrine of the baptism of the Spirit subsequent to salvation almost solely on the book of Acts.

But it is impossible to subscribe intelligently to the doctrine of the Spirit's baptizing work in the epistles of Paul and to confuse the Spirit's baptizing work with the enduement of power or an experience after salvation in the Acts of the Apostles. Yet it must be confessed that those who do so contend that their teaching does not conflict with the epistles. This, however, is not possible for a number of reasons.

First, any view of the baptizing work of the Holy Spirit in the gospels or the Acts must be reconciled with the central New Testament doctrinal passage on this subject in 1 Corinthians 12:13. To assert that John the Baptist's references to the term "baptized with the Holy Spirit" (Mt 3:11; Mk 1:8; Lk 3:16; Jn 1:33) and Jesus' allusion in Acts 1:5 do not pertain to the same thing as 1 Corinthians 12:13, when the subject of both is identical—namely, the baptizing work of the Holy Spirit—is an arbitrary assumption which has no basis in reason. Actually it violates sound exegetical method and can only result in ruling out a systematic biblical statement of the doctrine. Disconnecting Jesus' and John's predictive declaration of the Spirit's baptizing work from Paul's doctrinal exposition of it, the expositor produces a term that is being used other than as God's Word uses it.

The result of this error in practical outworking is only too evident. Although the Spirit's baptizing work may not directly be confused with a "second blessing," a "second work of grace," speaking in tongues, eradicationism, or some similar vagary, yet, in confounding it with the enduement of power, well-meaning expositors unwittingly cause confusion over the finished work of Christ and the believer's position and possessions in Him. They appropriate a term which, as the Pauline epistles show, *strictly* refers to the believer's unchanging *position* in Christ, and make it refer to that which is quite distinct— the believer's changing *experience* of Christ. James Cummings makes a thoughtful statement concerning the use of the term *baptism of the Spirit* in the light of the errors that cluster around it when he says: "The same thing as is signified by it may be dwelt on in language to which no such objections can be taken."[8]

Any view of the baptizing work of the Holy Spirit in the gospels and in the Acts must tally with the declaration in Ephesians 4:5 that there is in the church only one (spiritual) baptism.

If the spiritual baptism referred to by John the Baptist and Jesus is not identical with the spiritual baptizing of 1 Corinthians 12:13, there are in that case two distinct spiritual baptisms in Scripture. This, of course, cannot be; for the apostle most pointedly declares in listing the great foundational unities of the Christian faith that there is "one Lord, one faith, one baptism" (Eph 4:5). Incidentally, to construe this one baptism as water baptism would not harmonize with the context, which deals with spiritual truths: "one body . . . one Spirit . . . one hope . . . one Lord, one faith . . . one God and Father." Water baptism, as a ritual ceremony, is out of place in that company.

In the light of the baptizing work of the Holy Spirit, the term *baptism with the Holy Spirit* is not a correct and sound scriptural term for an *experience* of power. Rather it is always and only a term for a believer's *position* in Christ, which is the basis of his experience of power, but not itself the experience of the power.

Because the basis of the power is more fundamental than the reception of the power, Jesus was referring to this feature of the Spirit's work at Pentecost in Acts 1:5. Our Saviour was emphasizing the formation of His body, the church, by the Spirit rather than the empowering of the church for holy living and effective witnessing. The latter ministry of the Spirit created the high tide of spiritual life at Pentecost manifest in soul-winning, steadfastness in doctrine, fellowship, prayer, power, joy, praise (Ac 2:41-47), and is described by the words, "and they were all filled with the Holy Spirit" (Ac 2:4).

To fail to distinguish between the baptizing and filling work of the Holy Spirit at Pentecost leads to doctrinal confusion among God's people and may even lend shelter to the cults. The error of making "the baptism of the Spirit" an experience subsequent to regeneration, as René Pache says, "is the result of a confusion of terms."[9]

2. *Bible terminology for power is sound and gives no countenance to error or fanaticism.* To insist that the baptism with the Holy Spirit is not a correct Bible term for power is not to minimize the desperate need of the present-day church for power nor to deny the full availability of that power nor to lay discouragement in the way of God's people for claiming the fullness of that power.

Power is what the believer needs. Power is what he may have through his union with Christ by the baptizing work of the Spirit. Power is what he may have to the full by faith, if he will dare to believe he is what he is *in Christ* and thus translate the potential of that position into the dynamic of experience.

The Bible has an accurate and completely adequate vocabulary for the power the believer needs without his having to misuse the term "baptized with the Holy Spirit" to refer to this subject. Moreover, this expression, which is biblical enough, will never be redeemed from the abuse into which it has fallen until those who lament this abuse themselves cease to confuse it with an experience of power and use it *as the Scriptures use it*.

ENDUEMENT WITH POWER FROM ON HIGH

Several significant expressions are employed in the Word of God to describe the power of the Holy Spirit manifested at Pentecost. The first is *enduement with power from on high*. Our Lord told the disciples not to attempt any work or witness, but to "tarry," that is, stay or remain in Jerusalem until they should be "endued [clothed] with power from on high" (Lk 24:49). Christ's instructions directed them to be at the right place at the proper time when the Spirit would arrive according to the divine schedule.

The disciples followed Jesus' command and were present to receive the gift of the Holy Spirit and to welcome Him when He came. They were also endued with power from on high. But the enduement with power was only a part of the gift of the Spirit. The gift has now been received. The Holy Spirit has now come. The power from on high has now been vouchsafed to God's people upon the earth, and the enduement with power is the portion of all God's people to appropriate by faith.

The power from on high now permanently resides in the church, indwelling each believer individually. The power is the Person of the Spirit, who came at Pentecost.

Now there needs to be no ten-day waiting, no so-called tarrying for the power in connection with the gift of the Holy Spirit. Praying and waiting upon God have their necessary place. They serve the purpose that the Holy Spirit—who has already arrived, regenerated the believer, baptized him into vital union with Christ, sealed him to the day of redemption, and perpetually indwells him—may completely possess and fill him.

Since the Holy Spirit has been given, the power from on high is not only available here below but has its *source* in the believer, for the power is always the power of the Holy Spirit, and the Holy Spirit indwells every believer. If there is to be praying and waiting upon God in connection with the Holy Spirit and power, the purpose is not that God might give or pour out the Spirit, but that the Christian might *believe* that the Spirit has already been outpoured and thus remove any hindrances that may be blocking the Spirit from controlling and filling him and thereby manifesting His power.

Instead of the believer having to tarry for the Holy Spirit, the Holy Spirit is waiting upon the believer. John B. Kenyon aptly observes: "He has been tarrying through the years seeking to reveal Himself to you in His glory. Why do you keep Him waiting? The only occasion for you to tarry is that your heart may yield."[10]

Praying and waiting for the power of the Holy Spirit, then, are not so that God may do something with the Holy Spirit to the believer, but that the believer may believe that God has done all that needs to be done as far as the Holy Spirit and power are concerned, and to appropriate all the blessings and the dynamic of the outpoured Spirit. Since the Spirit in the believer is ever waiting and longing to fill him, any praying or waiting on the human side is to adjust the believer to the Holy Spirit within that He might fill him. The "power from on high" (Lk 24:49) now resides in the believer, since the Holy Spirit, who is that power, now indwells him.

Adjustment to the indwelling Spirit, which often requires waiting upon God in prayer because of sin and unyieldedness in the Christian's heart, insures the manifestation of God's power. But waiting upon God for the removal of hindrances to the manifestation of the indwelling Spirit's power is vastly different from "tarrying for the power from on high," as if the Holy Spirit had not come and the power were not the power of the Holy Spirit now resident in the Christian's heart.

POURING OUT OF THE SPIRIT

Another term used to describe the power of the Holy Spirit at Pentecost is contained in Peter's reference to Joel's prophecy: "But this is that which was spoken by the prophet Joel . . . *I will pour out of my Spirit*" (Ac 2:16, 17). Peter's description of the same copious effusion is more specific in the case of the Gentiles at Caesarea: "on the Gentiles also was poured out the gift of the Holy Ghost" (Ac 10:45). The figure of pouring out pictures the abundance of the Spirit's manifestation in the initial bestowment of the gift. All who were present at Pentecost and at Caesarea were mightily filled with the Spirit in addition to receiving the benefit of His other ministries included in the comprehensive term "the gift of the Holy Spirit" or the expression "they received the Holy Spirit" (Ac 8:17).

Similar in meaning to the figure of outpouring are the expressions "the Holy Spirit *fell on* . . . them" (Ac 10:44; 11:15) and "the Holy Spirit *came on* them" (Ac 19:6). In both cases the fullness of the Spirit in the original bestowment of the Spirit upon the Samaritans and upon the Gentiles is in view, and with it are connected the supernatural manifestations of tongues (Ac 10:44-46), perhaps also the wind and fire, as at Pentecost, although this is not definitely stated.

In other words, the giving of the gift of the Spirit and the advent of the Spirit to inaugurate the new age at Pentecost and to open that age to Samaritan (Ac 8) and Gentile (Ac 10) were attended with marvelous infillings. The gift was lavishly given and the arrival of the Spirit signally demonstrated in mighty infillings as well as miraculous wind, fire, and tongues.

FILLING OF THE SPIRIT

But by far the most important term for the power of the Spirit in the Acts (2:4; 4:8, 31; 9:17; 13:9, 52) and in the epistles is the expression *filled with the Spirit* (Eph 5:18).[11] It is the correct doctrinal term to be employed during this age in the light of the advent of the Spirit and the uniform teaching of the epistles.

It is not scripturally correct to use any of the other terms for power, such as "enduement from on high," "the pouring out," "the coming upon" or "receiving the Holy Spirit" to refer to a situation today of filling by the Holy Spirit. In their context in the gospels and the Acts these terms refer to the *initial* and *age-inaugurating* reception of the gift of the Holy Spirit by Jew, Samaritan and Gentile. Only as the terminology of Scripture is employed accurately will teaching on the subject of the Holy Spirit be redeemed from error. This means that doctrinal accuracy and soundness *must* precede experience.

The scriptural term *filled with the Spirit* stresses the continual need of being filled and keeping filled, in opposition to such erroneous notions as a second blessing, a second work of grace, eradication of the old nature and similar unsound ideas. As Joseph Parker observes: "Apostolic teaching will not allow men to settle down to the enjoyment of spiritual comfort as if sonship had no responsibilities."[12] There can be a danger in glorying over some experience rather than in Christ, a temptation to imagine onself to have had a blessing above other believers.

The expression *filled with the Spirit* avoids terminology that might obscure the finished work of Christ. The expression *baptized with the Holy Spirit* can have this obscuring effect. The Spirit's baptizing ministry relates to the believer's initial experience of salvation. To confuse this fundamental work of the Spirit, which forms the basis of the believer's position in Christ, can discredit the complete sufficiency of that work. Such confusion unavoidably opens the door to the misconceptions of second-blessing theology, which spring from a misunderstanding of the all-sufficiency of the atonement of Christ.

Only by strict adherence to biblical terminology can one be shielded from error and protect those whom he may teach. Insistence on the use of accurate terms is the only way to avoid being hindered by the use of unsound terminology and continually having to rid those expressions of the popular misconceptions associated with them. It is no accident that God's Word has given us a sound and completely adequate phrase, *filled with the Spirit*.

THE BIBLE PRESCRIPTION FOR POWER

1. *The Bible prescription for power calls for a knowledge of our position and possessions in Christ.*

Much of the powerlessness among Christians is because they are ignorant or poorly instructed about the truth of their position in Christ as the source of power. Consequently they are unable to appropriate the resources at their disposal as members of Christ. They cannot "be strong in the Lord" (Eph

6:10) because frequently they have only hazy ideas of what it means to be in the Lord. The bold assurance of the apostle Paul expressed in the conviction, "I can do all things through [or in] him who strengthens me" (Phil 4:13, NASB), is so often missing because of lack of knowledge of the new sphere into which they have been placed by the Spirit's baptizing work.

In the light of the importance of the believer's position in Christ as the basis of all his blessings, the emphasis the apostle places upon this phase of his teaching in his great doctrinal epistles, such as Ephesians, and his fervent prayers that believers might understand this glorious position in order to appropriate the power of it (Eph 1:15-23), is readily comprehensible. Without a knowledge of what we are in Christ, there can be no proper motivation to claim the power of the Holy Spirit nor any intelligent appropriation of that power.

2. *The Bible prescription for power requires faith to act upon our position and to claim our possessions.*

Knowledge in spiritual matters is necessary and serves as the basis upon which faith can act, but it is never presented in Scripture as sufficient in itself or as an end in itself. Faith must act upon knowledge of spiritual truth to convert it into experiential reality. Accordingly, Vaughn aptly describes such genuine or saving faith as "a principle by means of which the power of different kinds of truth is drawn out and thus becomes an instrument of sanctification . . . and a regulating force over character and action."[13] For the believer to profit by the teaching of the Word on the subject of his union with Christ, faith must lay hold of Bible doctrine and translate it into practical living. "Be ye doers of the word, and not hearers only, deceiving your own selves" (Ja 1:22). "If ye know these things, happy are ye if ye do them" (Jn 13:17).

Experiences of God's power, like all spiritual blessings, must be realized upon the principle of faith. "But without faith it is impossible to please him; for he that cometh to God must believe that he is, and that he is a rewarder of them that diligently seek him" (Heb 11:6). Since spiritual power is an extremely variable element, maintained only upon the continuous exercise of faith resulting in fulfilling certain conditions for the fullness of the Spirit, failure to exercise faith automatically involves failure to fulfill the requirements and results in less power.

The scriptural truth that power for victorious living and effective serving must be continuously nurtured by faith explains why "filled with the Spirit" is the correct biblical terminology for power. In the apostle's word to the Ephesians—"be ye filled with the Spirit"—is contained, as H.C.G. Moule properly emphasizes, "a precept not for a crisis but for the whole habit of the Christian's life."[14]

Inaccurate terms such as *the baptism with the Spirit, a second blessing,* and *a second definite experience* demonstrate their unsoundness by stressing an experience of infilling, but failing to indicate the necessity of maintaining that experience by a continual exercise of faith. As a result, many Christians are resting in some past infilling, erroneously described by some supposed scripturally accurate term. Wrong terminology beclouds the need for keeping filled and hinders from claiming a daily fresh anointing of God's power. To be filled with the Spirit "is to live at spiritual high tide, making immediate and normal recovery from every low-tide experience [and] it is constant obedience to the law of the Spirit."[15]

Other believers show their lack of sound instruction in the matter of the power of the Holy Spirit and an absence of true spirituality by imagining themselves to have had an experience placing them above their fellow Christians. Such notions, common in circles where a commendable stress is laid upon the necessity of the power of the Holy Spirit, nourish vanity and foster empty spiritual pride. Erroneous doctrines of this sort are only corrected by a return to the clear scriptural teaching that a Christian is under obligation not only to be filled with the Spirit, but to keep filled. This requires the continual exercise of faith in the believer's position in Christ, converting the benefits of that position into the power of daily experience. It also involves a strong belief in that which "all Scripture teaches," namely, the child of God's "entire dependence upon the Spirit of God."[16]

3. *The Bible prescription for power includes yieldedness to God's will and obedience to God's Word.*

The power of God for holy living and effective serving is not merely a matter of a rapturous experience so transforming and far-reaching in its effect, as erroneously to be called by some a second blessing, a second work of grace, or the baptism with the Holy Spirit. True, a crisis of surrender accompanied by the initial infilling of the Spirit is often characterized by an insurge of power and frequently by rapturous ecstasy. This is abundantly verified by the testimony and lives of well-known Christians in the present day and throughout the Christian centuries.

But the initial infilling of the Spirit, since it is only a beginning and not an end in itself, must not be misrepresented by terminology that suggests that the infilling is an end attained. Rather than the realization of an abundant life, it is the entrance into that life. The phrase "baptism with the Spirit" and other similar terminology have no concrete scriptural support as designations for the power of the Holy Spirit.

The Bible carefully avoids speaking about spiritual power in language that might imply that an experience of infilling, no matter how great or far-reaching in its effect, is to be considered as an end in itself. What might at first be construed as an exception is the initial bestowment of the gift of the Holy Spirit upon Jew, Samaritan, and Gentile to inaugurate the normal order of this age. This is only an apparent exception. Peculiar circumstances accompanied the initial coming of the Spirit, and they cannot legitimately be applied to the normal order of the age. Doctrinal teaching about the working of the Holy Spirit in filling and empowering the believer, now that the Spirit has come, is to be found in the epistles, not in the Acts. Sound exposition must reconcile the two.

For instance, "if some scriptures seem to indicate that the baptism of the Spirit is a blessing to be received subsequent to conversion, it is well to examine them carefully, noting the context, and asking, 'Was this spoken before or after Pentecost?'—

for the difference is immense; as a new dispensation began when the Holy Spirit descended to dwell in the believer."[17]

In the doctrinal epistles, since "spiritual power . . . is conditioned by adjustment,"[18] both the necessity of a once-for-all surrender to God's will as well as a continuous yielding on the basis of the comprehensive act are stressed. The one is essential to enter upon the experience of fullness of power, and the other is mandatory for the continuance of the manifestation of the fullness. In Romans 12:1 the call is to the comprehensive act: "I beseech you therefore, brethren, by the mercies of God, that ye present [yield] your bodies a living sacrifice, holy, acceptable unto God, which is your reasonable service." The same once-for-all yielding to God is in view in Romans 6:13: "Neither yield ye your members as instruments of unrighteousness unto sin: but yield yourselves unto God." Similarly, in Romans 6:19 the exhortation is to "yield your members servants to righteousness unto holiness."

Everywhere in the epistles, a continual yielding on the basis of a previous once-for-all surrender is assumed. Quite plainly the apostle warns that a continuous surrender to God is necessary to serve Him. "Know ye not, that to whom ye yield yourselves servants to obey" [a continuous yielding is indicated here] his servants ye are to whom ye obey: whether of sin unto death, or of obedience unto righteousness?" (Ro 6:16). "Being then made free from sin, ye became the servants of righteousness" (Ro 6:18).

The frequent figure of walking (Gal 5:16; Eph 4:1) presupposes unbroken submission to God's will. The apostle closely connects the knowledge of God's will and the submission to His purpose with the injunction to be continually filled with the Spirit. "See then that ye walk circumspectly, not as fools, but as wise, redeeming the time, because the days are evil. Wherefore be not unwise, but understanding what the will of the Lord is. And be not drunk with wine, wherein is excess; but be filled with the Spirit" (Eph 5:15-18).

Yieldedness to God's will makes possible obedience to God's Word, and both are essential to the enjoyment of God's power.

The Holy Spirit leads the believer first to separate himself from everything that is evil and then inspires and energizes him in everything that is good. If the believer refuses to follow the Word in the matter of separation from evil, the Holy Spirit is grieved (Eph 4:30). If he declines to obey the Word and to perform that which is good, the Holy Spirit is quenched (1 Th 5:19). To be filled with the Spirit the believer must perseveringly avoid grieving the Spirit in the matter of complicity with evil and quenching Him in failing to be obedient in the matter of the performance of every good work.[19]

The Spirit of God always leads the yielded believer to the Word, to study it, meditate upon it, and obey it, in order to be cleansed and directed in the pathway of power by it. S. D. Gordon lists what he aptly calls "three laws of continuance of power." The first, "obey"; the second, "obey the book of God as interpreted by the Spirit of God"; the third, "time alone with the book daily."[20] It is impossible to be Spirit-filled and empowered by God without day by day studying to show oneself "approved unto God, a workman that needeth not to be ashamed, rightly dividing the word of truth" (2 Ti 2:15). Yieldedness to God's will and obedience to God's Word are indispensable conditions for being kept filled with the Spirit.

4. *The Bible prescription for power comprehends the exercise of prevailing prayer.*

It is just as impossible for a believer to remain Spirit-filled and not engage in prevailing prayer as it is for him to become Spirit-filled and not be yielded to God's will and obedient to God's Word. The Spirit-filled experience is the signal for Satanic opposition. God's power in the life *always* arouses the devil's power of temptation and attack. The Spirit-directed walk of the child of God is bound to merge into a warfare. Because of the triple onslaught of the world, the flesh, and the devil, "the Christian pilgrim must also be the soldier of Christ, as he walks, prepared also to war."[21]

The classic passage describing the inevitable prayer conflict of the Spirit-filled believer against the powers of darkness is Ephesians 6:10-20. In the first three chapters of the Ephesian

letter, the apostle Paul outlines the exalted position of the believer "in the heavenlies in Christ." In the last three chapters
he describes the holy walk of the Spirit-filled believer on earth,
consonant with his position "in the heavenlies in Christ (Eph
4:1—6:9). As walk of necessity merges into war (Eph 6:10),
the apostle mentions first what is of primary importance; namely, the believer's strength for the conflict derived from his relationship to the Lord as a result of the baptizing work of the
Spirit. "Be strong in the Lord" (v. 10), or as H. C. G. Moule
renders it, "strengthen yourselves always in the Lord," pointing
out that "the verb is in the present tense and suggests a continual 'strengthening.' "[22] It is important to note also that the
strengthening is such "as can take effect only in union with
Christ."[23]

Realizing we are what we are in Christ (Ro 6:1-10) and
reckoning upon our position of union (Ro 6:11) is the ground
of our victory and the source of our power over the enemy
(Eph 6:12). Just as reckoning ourselves "dead indeed unto
sin and alive unto God through [in union with] Christ" is a
present tense and must involve the continuous exercise of faith,
so the strengthening in Ephesians 6:10 is a present tense and involves the same unceasing activity of faith.

> Triumphant conquest upon a principle of *faith* is ever the
> one responsibility of the believer. A Christian is not appointed
> to fight his foes single-handed and alone; he is to fight the
> "good fight of faith"! Thus the Apostle could say at the end
> of his life of wonderful service, "I have fought a good fight"
> (2 Tim. 4:7), learning, as he had, how to perform that which
> is good (Rom. 7:18). To be "strong in the Lord and in the
> power of his might" calls for an unceasing dependence upon
> God, in which dependence all confidence in self is abandoned.
> The conflict is not a crisis-experience wherein the deliver-
> ance is won in a moment of time forever; it is rather to "walk
> by means of the Spirit" (Gal. 5:16-18), and there can be
> no more expressive term employed than to liken this unceas-
> ing conflict to a *walk* by means of the Spirit.[24]

Having described the believer's strength for the prayer conflict, the apostle indicates his equipment against the foe, which

is the full armor provided by God (Eph 6:11-17). The divine provision of the armor is necessitated by the spiritual nature of the foe (v. 12). "Wherefore, take unto you the whole armor of God" (v. 13). "Take," not "make," is the Spirit's direction. God has made the panoply, a perfect product of His redemptive grace. We have only to put it on and keep it on to be able to stand against our foe and "having done all, to stand."

"Stand therefore!" That is what God asks of the believer. We are to stand as the victors we are—stand in the victory of Calvary. God has provided His spiritual armor primarily to protect what is dearest to Him on earth because it is united to His Son, who is dearest to Him in heaven—the church, Christ's body, "the fulness of him that filleth all in all" (Eph 1:23).

The apostle, having set forth the Christian warrior's strength and equipment against the enemy, concludes with an indication of the employment of the resources in prevailing prayer (Eph 6:18-20). "Praying always with all prayer and supplication in the Spirit, and watching thereunto with all perseverance for all saints" (v. 18). Prayer in the conflict is not to be viewed as a part of the warrior's resources or equipment, or as "another weapon," as John Bunyan sees it when he asserts that Christian "was forced to put up his sword, and betake himself to another weapon, called All-Prayer."[25] All-Prayer is *the employment of the panoply provided by God.*

"Prayer is naturally connected with action."[26] It is the believer's appropriation of the resources of strength he has in Christ and his using the equipment provided for him in his aggressive stand against evil.

Only through prayer, which is "of all sorts," "at all seasons," "for all saints," "with all perseverance and supplication," and "in the Spirit," can the believer utilize the strength which is his in the Lord. Only thus can he put on the armor of God, and "stand" as a Spirit-filled and Spirit-empowered warrior. If he is to obey the injunction to keep on being filled with the Spirit (Eph 5:18), he must always be ready to enter the conflict of prayer in this life, for the Christian never reaches "a stage when there is no more conflict, and no performance of God's will without the consciousness of inward opposition."[27]

But Spirit-filled prayer is prevailing prayer in which the foe is vanquished and the victory won not only for the believer himself but also by intercession for others (Eph 6:19, 20). When the believer—apprehending his position of oneness with his Lord and acting upon that position by faith in yielding himself to God in obedience to the Word—is filled with the Spirit, the full onslaught of the powers of darkness is directed against him, pressing him to abandon his impregnable fortress and to yield to pressure at some point.

But the Christian warrior, steadfastly refusing to surrender the ground which is his in Christ and availing himself of the full armor of God, maintains his Spirit-filled experience. He is therefore invincible. The power of God in his life, as he is thus protected through Satanic temptation and attack, now becomes available for an effectual ministry, bringing blessing to men and glory to God.

It must be remembered that this is the way God's power operates. There are no short cuts, no experiences to be rested in, no breaking of spiritual laws. "All power is conditioned."[28] Power in the natural world is conditioned and operates under certain definite laws. So spiritual power is subject to conditions and the laws of the spiritual realm. Spiritual experiences there will be—crises of surrender, and infillings of the Spirit. But these must be carefully nurtured and maintained as an abiding experience and not carried over as a relic of a spiritual past or employed as a substitute for present spiritual vitality.

A. B. Simpson's words are to the point.

> There was a time when the Holy Ghost's heavenly fire was a mysterious force, flashing, like lightning in the skies, we knew not why or whither; coming now upon a Moses, and again upon an Elijah; sometimes falling, as at Carmel in awful majesty upon the altar of sacrifice; sometimes striking, as in Israel's camp, in the destroying flame of God's anger; sometimes appearing in the burning bush at Horeb, as the strange mysterious symbol of Jehovah's presence.
>
> But since Christ's ascension the Holy Spirit has condescended to dwell amongst us under certain plainly-revealed laws, and to place at our service and command all the forces

and resources of His power, according to definite, simple and regular laws of operation, in accordance with which the simplest disciple can use Him for the needs of his life and work just as easily as we use the force of electricity for the business of life. He has even been pleased to call Himself "the law of the Spirit of life in Christ Jesus."[29]

God grant that we as believers, brought into living oneness with our risen and ascended Lord through the baptism of the Holy Spirit, may so constantly accommodate ourselves to the law of the Spirit of life in Christ Jesus that the power of God may not only fill us but remain upon us for holy living and effective serving. Then men will begin to see in experience something of the glory of the position that is the possession of all who are "in Christ."

Notes

CHAPTER 1

1. For example, see Don Basham, *A Handbook on Holy Spirit Baptism,* pp. 10, 18-27; R. L. Brandt, "The Case for Speaking in Tongues," *Pentecostal Evangel* 48 (1960): 4, 29-30.
2. For the nature of glossolalia in Pentecostal interpretation, see Frederick Dale Bruner, *A Theology of the Holy Spirit,* pp. 85-86; 144-45.
3. See Donald G. Bloesch, "The Charismatic Revival: A Theological Critique," *Religion in Life* 35 (1966): 364-80.
4. *The Word of God on the Baptism of the Holy Ghost,* tract 4286 (Springfield, Mo.: Gospel Pub. House, n.d.).
5. Bruner, p. 37. On the Methodist origins of Pentecostalism, see also Nils Bloch-Hoell, *The Pentecostal Movement: Its Origin, Development, and Distinctive Character,* p. 128.
6. John Wesley, *A Plain Account of Christian Perfection,* p. 24.
7. Charles Finney, *Memoirs,* pp. 20-21, 55, 65, 95.
8. Cited by William G. McLoughlin, Jr., *Modern Revivalism: Charles Grandison Finney to Billy Graham,* pp. 86-87.
9. Ibid., p. 66.
10. See Elmer T. Clark, *The Small Sects of America,* rev. ed., p. 72.
11. Claude Kendrick, *The Promise Fulfilled: A History of the Modern Pentecostal Movement,* p. 33.
12. W. E. Boardman, *The Higher Christian Life,* p. 47.
13. Ibid., p. 76.
14. Charles Conn, *Pillars of Pentecost,* p. 27; see also J. T. Nichols, *Pentecostalism,* pp. 5-7.
15. R. A. Torrey, *What the Bible Teaches: A Thorough and Comprehensive Study of What the Bible Has to Say Concerning the Great Doctrines of Which It Treats,* p. 271.
16. Ibid.
17. Bloch-Hoell, pp. 75-86.
18. Elmer T. Clark, "Pentecostal Churches," in *The Twentieth Century Encyclopedia of Religious Knowledge,* p. 865.
19. Kevin and Dorothy Ranaghan, *Catholic Pentecostals.*
20. For the rise of Neo-Pentecostalism, see John Sherrill, *They Speak with Other Tongues;* and Michael Harper, *As at the Beginning: The Twentieth Century Pentecostal Revival.*
21. Anthony Hoekema, *Holy Spirit Baptism,* p. 58.
22. See Laurence Christenson, *Speaking in Tongues and Its Significance for the Church.*
23. For exhaustive evidence of this statement, see Frederick Dale Bruner, *A Theology of the Holy Spirit* (note 2 above); and James Dunn's massive study, *The Baptism in the Holy Spirit.* Bruner's monumental work is subtitled, *The Pentecostal Experience and the New Testament Witness.* Dunn's work is subtitled *A Reexamination of the New Testament Teaching on the Gift of the Spirit in Relation to Pentecostalism Today.*

173

24. See Bruner, pp. 63-69; Dunn, pp. 38-102; and Merrill F. Unger, *The New Testament Teaching on Tongues,* pp. 14-73.
25. See Bloch-Hoell, p. 175.
26. Guy P. Duffield, Jr., *Pentecostal Preaching,* pp. 15-16.
27. See the Pentecostal theologian, Ernest S. Williams, *Systematic Theology,* 3:47.
28. Donald Gee, *Pentecost* 45 (September 1958): 17. See also Gee, *The Pentecostal Movement,* pp. 7-8. See also article 8 of The Statement of Fundamental Truths of the Assemblies of God: "The Baptism of believers in the Holy Ghost is witnessed by the initial physical sign of speaking in tongues."
29. Howard M. Erwin, *These Are Not Drunken, As Ye Suppose,* p. 105.
30. Christenson, p. 55.
31. Ibid., pp. 55-56.
32. Ranaghan, p. 222.
33. Ibid., p. 221.
34. See Francis A. Schaeffer, "Beware of the New Super-Spirituality," *Eternity,* November 1972, pp. 15-17, 36, 38; Vernon C. Grounds, "Understanding the Neo-Mystical Movement," *Christian Heritage Magazine,* January 1973, pp. 4-7.

CHAPTER 2

1. G. Campbell Morgan, *The Spirit of God,* p. 169.
2. Lewis Sperry Chafer, *Salvation,* pp. 59-67.
3. See J. Gilchrist Lawson's *Deeper Experiences of Famous Christians.* The Pentecostal leader Ralph Riggs, commenting on Lawson's book, says, "It is good to know that the Baptism in the Spirit is more than a Scriptural doctrine: it is an experience into which many prominent Christian workers have actually entered, some in recent generations (*The Spirit Himself,* p. 100.)
4. T. J. McCrossan, *Christ's Paralyzed Church X-Rayed,* pp. 25-100.
5. George P. Pardington, *The Crisis of the Deeper Life,* p. 164.
6. R. A. Torrey, *The Baptism with the Holy Spirit,* pp. 13, 14.
7. For the rise of Neo-Pentecostalism, see John Sherrill, *They Speak with Other Tongues;* and Michael Harper, *As at the Beginning: The Twentieth Century Pentecostal Revival.* For Neo-Pentecostalism as a movement in Romanism, see Kevin and Dorothy Ranaghan, *Catholic Pentecostals.*
8. Louis Bauman, *The Modern Tongues Movement,* pp. 1-38.
9. Ernest Williams, "Your Questions," *Pentecostal Evangel* 49 (January 1961): 11. See John T. Nichols, *Pentecostalism,* pp. 1-2.
10. H. E. Dana and J. R. Mantey, *A Manual Grammar of the Greek New Testament,* p. 195.
11. C. I. Scofield, *Rightly Dividing the Word of Truth,* p. 74.
12. J. H. Thayer, *Greek-English Lexicon of the New Testament,* s.v. "gift of grace."
13. See the Pentecostal writers Ralph M. Riggs, *The Spirit Himself,* pp. 102-112; and Donald Gee, *God's Great Gift,* pp. 55, 57.
14. I. M. Haldeman, *Holy Ghost or Water?,* p. 4.
15. Edmund B. Fairfield, *Letters on Baptism,* pp. 32-122.
16. James W. Dale, *Judaic Baptism,* p. 400.
17. James W. Dale, *Johannic Baptism,* p. 417.
18. E. E. Hawes, *Baptism Mode Studies,* pp. 81-109.
19. James W. Dale, *Christic and Patristic Baptism,* pp. 162-240.
20. See Paul Van Gorder, *Cure for Charismatic Confusion,* pp. 1-20; Merrill F. Unger, *New Testament Teaching on Tongues,* pp. 1-13.
21. See the Pentecostal Riggs, *The Spirit Himself,* pp. 55-56. Riggs posits a baptism of penitents into the body of Christ at conversion and the subsequent baptism of believers by Christ into the Holy Spirit (Pentecost experience).
22. Lewis Sperry Chafer, "Careless Misstatements of Vital Truth," *Our Hope* 30 (March 1924): 11.

CHAPTER 3

1. A. C. Gaebelein, *The Annotated Bible*, vol. 1, *The Pentateuch*, p. 267.
2. S. Ridout, *The Person and Work of the Holy Spirit*, p. 12.
3. W. T. P. Wolston, *Another Comforter*, pp. 24, 95f.
4. Allen B. Webb, *The Presence and Office of the Holy Spirit*, p. 44.
5. Wolston, p. 21.
6. Ridout, p. 30.
7. John Owen, *A Discourse Concerning the Holy Spirit*, 1:211.
8. George Soltau, *The Person and Mission of the Holy Spirit*, pp. 78-79.
9. René Pache, *The Person and Work of the Holy Spirit*, p. 73.
10. Ibid., p. 76.
11. See Lewis Sperry Chafer, *Systematic Theology*, 4:268 ff.; 5:328 ff.
12. Ibid., 5:300.
13. Clarence Larkin, *Dispensational Truth*, p. 58.
14. J. F. Strombeck, *First the Rapture*, p. 102; Chafer, 4:372 ff.
15. John F. Walvoord, *The Doctrine of the Holy Spirit*, pp. 159-62.
16. See Anthony A. Hoekema, *Holy Spirit Baptism*, pp. 17-18; James G. Dunn, *Baptism in the Holy Spirit*, p. 25; and R. A. Finlayson, "Baptism of the Holy Spirit," in *The Encyclopedia of Christianity*, p. 538.
17. See E. H. Plumptre, *A New Testament Commentary for English Readers*, 1:12.
18. R. A. Torrey, *The Baptism with the Holy Spirit*, p. 17; F. M. Ellis in *The Person and Ministry of the Holy Spirit*, p. 126 f.
19. Walvoord, p. 165. Raymond E. Brown notes that the baptism with the Spirit "is a beneficial cleansing, while baptism with fire is a destructive purgation (Isa iv 4)" (*The Anchor Bible*, vol. 29, *The Gospel of John*, p. 57).
20. A. C. Gaebelein, *The Gospel of Matthew*, p. 71.
21. For example, Henry W. Frost, *Who Is the Holy Spirit?* (New York: Fleming Revell, 1938), p. 57.
22. Torrey, p. 27.
23. See R. C. Hicks, *The Baptism of Jesus*, for a full discussion of this subject; also James W. Dale, *Christic and Patristic Baptism*.
24. Chafer, 5:65.
25. Ibid., 6:72.
26. Ibid., pp. 130 ff. For the bearing of our Lord's upper room teaching on the second-blessing and Pentecostal views, see Dale Bruner, *A Theology of the Holy Spirit*, pp. 278-80.
27. Chafer, 6:125.
28. Merrill C. Tenney, *John: The Gospel of Belief* (Grand Rapids: Eerdmans, 1948), p. 135.
29. Leon Morris, "Gospel of John," in *The New International Commentary on the New Testament*, pp. 152-53.
30. Wolston, pp. 102 f.
31. G. Campbell Morgan, *The Spirit of God*, pp. 181-82.
32. Chafer, 5:145.

CHAPTER 4

1. W. H. Griffith Thomas, *The Holy Spirit of God*, p. 40.
2. For a synoptic statement of the significance of Pentecost, see *Unger's Bible Handbook*, pp. 569-70.
3. L. S. Chafer, *Salvation*, pp. 59-67; see also Chafer, *Systematic Theology*, 3:55-115.
4. For the difference between Pentecostal and other evangelical Christians in the holiness category of believers because of the distinctive Pentecostal doctrine of Spirit baptism, see Guy P. Duffield, Jr., *Pentecostal Preaching*, pp. 15-16.

5. G. Campbell Morgan, *The Acts of the Apostles*, p. 29.
6. See the Pentecostals Charles W. Conn, *Pillars of Pentecost*, pp. 96-104; and Ralph M. Riggs, *The Spirit Himself*, 4: 102-12.
7. Frederick Dale Bruner, *A Theology of the Holy Spirit*, p. 201.
8. Merrill F. Unger, *The Baptizing Work of the Holy Spirit*, p. 59.
9. R. A. Torrey, *The Baptism with the Holy Spirit*, pp. 9, 10.
10. Bruner, p. 45.
11. Donald Gee, *The Pentecostal Movement*, pp. 4-5.
12. See Bruner, pp. 153-319. With brilliant analysis Bruner examines the Pentecostal claims in the light of the New Testament witness. See also Merrill F. Unger, *The Baptizing Work of the Holy Spirit*, pp. 77-136.
13. See John R. Stott, *The Baptism and Fullness of the Spirit*, pp. 7-60. See also Thomas O. Figart, "The Filling of the Spirit," *Christian Victory Magazine*, April 1973, pp. 48-51.
14. A. C. Gaebelein, *The Annotated Bible*, vol. 1, New Testament, p. 259.
15. James B. Green, *Studies in the Holy Spirit*, p. 79.
16. T. J. McCrossan, *Christ's Paralyzed Church X-Rayed*, pp. 55-86.
17. Cornelius Stam, *The Fundamentals of Dispensationalism*, pp. 233-47; see also H. A. Ironside, *Wrongly Dividing the Word of Truth*, pp. 9-10.
18. For a full discussion of tongues, see Merrill F. Unger, *The New Testament Teaching on Tongues*, particularly pp. 27-34; see also Donald W. Burdick, *Tongues: To Speak or Not to Speak*, pp. 1-89.
19. Ralph M. Riggs, *The Spirit Himself*, p. 109.
20. Thomas B. Barratt, *When the Fire Fell*, p. 115.

CHAPTER 5

1. G. Campbell Morgan, *The Acts of the Apostles*, p. 263.
2. See *Young's Concordance*, p. 390.
3. For example, E. J. Jarvis, "This Is That," *Pentecostal Evangel* 49 (January 1961):7.
4. Frederic Dale Bruner, *The Theology of the Holy Spirit*, p. 192.
5. Lewis Sperry Chafer, *Systematic Theology*, 6:132.
6. See Bruner, pp. 193-94.
7. For a full discussion of the significance of tongues in Acts, see Merrill F. Unger, *The New Testament Teaching on Tongues*, pp. 27-78. See Bruner, pp. 162-65, 168, 179-81. See James Dunn, *Baptism in the Holy Spirit*, pp. 38-82; Robert G. Gromacki, *The Modern Tongues Movement;* Donald Burdick, *Tongues: To Speak or Not to Speak*, pp. 13-18.
8. See Zane C. Hodges, "The Purpose of Tongues," *Bibliotheca Sacra*, July-September 1963, pp. 226-33; S. Lewis Johnson, "The Gift of Tongues in the Book of Acts," *Bibliotheca Sacra*, October-December 1963, pp. 308-31.
9. Bruner, p. 192. So Otto Dibelius, *Die Werdende Kirche: Eine Einführung in die Apostelgeschichte*, p. 103.
10. Bruner, p. 192.
11. R. J. Knowling, *The Acts of the Apostles*, in The Expositor's Greek New Testament, p. 403.
12. A. T. Robertson, *Grammar of the Greek New Testament in the Light of Historical Research*, p. 1113.
13. Ibid., pp. 860-61.
14. C. I. Scofield, *New Scofield Reference Bible*, note on Acts 19:2, p. 1175.

CHAPTER 6

1. James W. Dale, *Classic Baptism* (Philadelphia: Presby. Brd. of Publn., 1867), p. 354.

2. Cf. the Pentecostal Ray H. Hughes, who denies that 1 Co 12:13 refers to Spirit baptism, but maintains it refers simply to the agency of the Spirit in unifying the body of Christ, *What Is Pentecost?* (Cleveland, Tenn.: Pathway, 1968), p. 23.

3. H. E. Dana and J. R. Mantey, *A Manual Grammar of the Greek New Testament* (New York: Macmillan, 1939), p. 105.

4. See Anthony Hoekema, *Holy Spirit Baptism*, pp. 21-22.

5. See G. R. Beasley-Murray, "The Holy Spirit, Baptism, and the Body of Christ," *Review and Expositor* 63 (1966):181.

6. Lewis Sperry Chafer, *Systematic Theology*, 6:143.

7. Even Frederick Dale Bruner in his otherwise brilliant assessment of the Pentecostal error fails to make a clear distinction on this vital point. See *A Theology of the Holy Spirit*, p. 294.

8. Bruner ably points this out, p. 244.

9. Ibid., pp. 241-44.

10. John F. Walvoord, *The Doctrine of the Holy Spirit*, p. 156.

11. See the doctrinal definition of the baptism of the Holy Spirit as understood by the Assemblies of God, the largest North American Pentecostal body, as recorded by Irwin Winehouse, *The Assemblies of God: A Popular Survey*, pp. 207-9.

12. Ray C. Stedman, "One Baptism," *Our Hope Magazine* 59 (1952): 298.

13. Walvoord, p. 157.

14. F. J. Huegel, *Bone of His Bone*, pp. 57-62.

15. René Pache, *The Person and Work of the Holy Spirit*, pp. 75-76.

16. Frederic Rendall, "The Epistle to the Galatians," in *The Expositor's Greek New Testament*, ed. William Robertson Nicoll, 3:174.

17. Merrill F. Unger, *Unger's Bible Handbook*, p. 661.

CHAPTER 7

1. Frederick Dale Bruner, *A Theology of the Holy Spirit*, pp. 264-65.

2. See G. R. Beasley-Murray, *Baptism in the New Testament*, pp. 126-46; 276-77. R. E. O. White, *The Biblical Doctrine of Initiation* (London: Hodder and Stoughton, 1960), pp. 217, 273, 280.

3. Bruner, p. 264.

4. See John F. Walvoord, *The Doctrine of the Holy Spirit*, pp. 154-55.

5. F. F. Bruce and E. K. Simpson, *Commentary on the Epistles to the Ephesians and Colossians*, p. 87.

6. For a study of the modern ecumenical trend, see W. A. Visser t'Hooft, *The Meaning of Ecumenical; R. Rouse and S. C. Neill, eds., A History of the Ecumenical Movement 1517-1948;* S. C. Neill, *Towards Church Union 1937-1952; The Ecumenical Review,* 1948-1970; *The Church, the Churches, and the World Council of Churches,* by the Central Committee of the World Council of Churches (1950).

7. See Merrill F. Unger, *Demons in the World Today*, pp. 147-75. See also Kurt Koch, *Revival Fires in Canada*, particularly chapter entitled "Pseudo-Charismatic Movements," pp. 71-75.

8. See E. Schuyler English, *Studies in the Epistle to the Colossians*, p. 71.

9. Alfred Barry, "The Epistles to the Ephesians, Philippians, and Colossians," in *Ephesians to Revelation*, p. 107.

10. G. R. Beasley-Murray, "The Holy Spirit, Baptism, and the Body of Christ," *Review and Expositor* 63 (Spring 1966): 182.

11. Cited by Kurt D. Schmidt, "Luthers Lehre vom Heiligen Geist," in *Schrift und Bekenntnis: Zeugnisse Lutherischer Theologie*, p. 157.

12. See Bruce and Simpson, p. 234.

13. Lewis Sperry Chafer, *Systematic Theology*, 6:192-93.

14. Ibid., p. 146.

15. Bruce and Simpson, p. 235.
16. Robert Jamieson, A. R. Fausset, and D. Brown, *A Commentary on the Old and New Testaments*, 2:509.
17. Chafer, p. 150.

CHAPTER 8

1. For the Pentecostal distinction between the gift and the gifts of the Spirit, see Melvin L. Hodges, *Spiritual Gifts*, pp. 4, 15-16.
2. Donald Gee, *Concerning Spiritual Gifts: A Series of Bible Studies*, p. 15.
3. Merrill F. Unger, *The Baptizing Work of the Holy Spirit*, p. 112, also pp. 53-76.
4. Gee, p. 10. See also Guy P. Duffield, *Pentecostal Preaching*, p. 53; Carl Bromback, *What Meaneth This?*, p. 61.
5. Laurence Christenson, *Speaking in Tongues and Its Significance for the Church*, p. 117.
6. Kevin and Dorothy Ranaghan, *Catholic Pentecostals*, p. 160.
7. Harold Horton, *The Gifts of the Spirit*, p. 39.
8. For a thorough and well-documented discussion of this, see B. B. Warfield, *Counterfeit Miracles*, pp. 1-31. See also J. S. McEwen, *Scottish Journal of Theology* 7 (1954): 133-52.
9. Theodore Epp, "The Bible or Experience," *Christian Victory Magazine* 47 (April 1973): 14.

CHAPTER 9

1. See John R. Rice, *The Power of Pentecost or the Fullness of the Spirit*, pp. 150, 152.
2. Charles R. Erdman, *The Spirit of Christ*, p. 47.
3. W. H. Griffith Thomas, *Grace and Power*, p. 35.
4. Rice, pp. 149-52.
5. See P. Kluepfel, *The Holy Spirit in the Life and Teachings of Jesus and the Early Church*, p. 86; William E. Biederwolf, *A Help to the Study of the Holy Spirit*, p. 54; R. A. Torrey, *The Baptism with the Holy Spirit*, pp. 63-65.
6. Abraham Kuyper, *The Work of the Holy Spirit*, p. 115.
7. H. K. Downie, *Harvest Festivals*, p. 91.
8. James Cummings, *Through the Eternal Spirit: A Biblical Study on the Holy Ghost*, p. 122.
9. René Pache, *The Person and Work of the Holy Spirit*, p. 74.
10. John B. Kenyon, *The Bible Revelation of the Holy Spirit*, p. 138.
11. For an exhaustive exposition of this term, see John Goodwin, *A Being Filled with the Spirit*, pp. 1-492.
12. Joseph Parker, *The Paraclete: The Holy Ghost*, p. 170.
13. C. R. Vaughn, *The Gifts of the Holy Spirit to Unbelievers and Believers*, p. 127.
14. H. C. G. Moule, *Veni, Creator*, p. 216.
15. J. C. Massee, *The Holy Spirit*, p. 119.
16. William Law, *The Power of the Spirit: An Address to the Clergy, with Additional Extracts from the Writings of William Law*, p. 33.
17. H. A. Ironside, *The Mission of the Holy Spirit*, p. 33.
18. F. J. Miles, *The Greatest Unused Power in the World*, p. 73.
19. H. D. Dolman, *Simple Talks on the Holy Spirit*, pp. 154-59.
20. S. D. Gordon, *Quiet Talks on Power*, pp. 164-68.
21. Norman B. Harrison, *His Very Own*, p. 151; see also F. F. Bruce and E. K. Simpson, *Commentary on the Epistles to the Ephesians and Colossians*, pp. 142-43.
22. H. C. G. Moule, *Ephesian Studies*, p. 323.

23. S. D. F. Salmond, "The Epistle to the Ephesians," in *The Expositor's Greek Testament*, 3:382.
24. Lewis Sperry Chafer, *The Ephesian Letter*, p. 162.
25. John Bunyan, *Pilgrim's Progress*, p. 63.
26. Brooke Foss Westcott, *Saint Paul's Epistle to the Ephesians*, p. 97.
27. George Smeaton, *The Doctrine of the Holy Spirit*, p. 229.
28. F. J. Miles, p. 73.
29. A. B. Simpson, *The Holy Spirit or Power from on High*, pp. 116-17.

Bibliography

Barratt, Thomas B. *When the Fire Fell.* Oslo: Hansen & Sonner, 1927.

Barry, Alfred. "The Epistles to the Ephesians, Philippians, and Colossians." *Ephesians to Revelation,* ed. C. J. Ellicott. Ellicott's Commentary on the Whole Bible, Vol. 8. Grand Rapids: Zondervan, n.d.

Basham, Don. *A Handbook on Holy Spirit Baptism.* Monroeville, Pa.: Whitaker Books, 1969.

Bauman, Louis S. *The Modern Tongues Movement.* Long Beach, Calif.: Alan Pearce, 1925.

Beasley-Murray, G. R. *Baptism in the New Testament.* London: Macmillan, 1962.

———. "The Holy Spirit, Baptism, and the Body of Christ." *Review and Expositor* 63 (Spring 1966): 177-85.

Biederwolf, William E. *A Help to the Study of the Holy Spirit.* Grand Rapids: Zondervan, 1936.

Bloch-Hoell, Nils. *The Pentecostal Movement: Its Origin, Development, and Distinctive Character.* Oslo: Universitetsforlaget, 1964.

Bloesch, Donald G. "The Charismatic Revival: A Theological Critique," *Religion in Life* 35 (Summer 1966): 364-80.

Boardman, W. E. *The Higher Christian Life.* Boston: Henry Hoyt, 1859.

Brandt, R. L. "The Case for Speaking in Tongues." *Pentecostal Evangel* 48 (1960).

Bromback, Carl. *What Meaneth This?* Springfield, Mo.: Gospel Pub., 1947.

Brown, Raymond E. *The Anchor Bible,* vol. 29. *The Gospel According to John.* Ed. W. F. Albright and D. N. Freedman. New York: Doubleday, 1966, 1970.

Bruce, F. F., and Simpson, E. K. *Commentary on the Epistles to the Ephesians and Colossians.* The New International Commentary on the New Testament, ed. F. F. Bruce. Grand Rapids: Eerdmans, 1957.

Bruner, Frederick Dale. *A Theology of the Holy Spirit: The Pentecostal Experience and the New Testament Witness.* Grand Rapids: Eerdmans, 1970.

Bunyan, John. *The Pilgrim's Progress.* New York: Cassell, Petter, Galpin, n.d.

Burdick, Donald W. *Tongues: To Speak or Not to Speak.* Chicago: Moody, 1969.

Chafer, Lewis Sperry. *Salvation.* Wheaton, Ill.: Van Kampen, 1940.

————. *Major Bible Themes.* Wheaton, Ill.: Van Kampen, 1942.

————. *Systematic Theology.* Vols. 1-8. Dallas: Dallas Sem., 1948.

————. *The Kingdom in History and Prophecy.* Wheaton, Ill.: Van Kampen, 1936.

————. "Careless Misstatements of Vital Truth." *Our Hope* 30 (1924):540-51.

————. *He That Is Spiritual.* Wheaton, Ill.: Van Kampen, 1940.

————. *The Ephesian Letter.* New York: Loizeaux, 1935.

Christenson, Laurence. *Speaking in Tongues and Its Significance for the Church.* Minneapolis: Bethany Fellowship, 1968.

Clark, Elmer T. *The Small Sects of America.* Nashville, Tenn.: Abingdon-Cokesbury, 1949.

————. "Pentecostal Churches." *Twentieth Century Encyclopedia of Religious Knowledge.* Grand Rapids: Baker, 1955.

Conn, Charles. *Pillars of Pentecost.* Cleveland, Tenn.: Pathway, 1956.

Cummings, James E. *Through the Eternal Spirit: A Biblical Study on the Holy Ghost.* New York: Revell, 1896.

Dale, James W. *Judaic Baptism.* Philadelphia: Wm. Rutter, 1871.

————. *Johannic Baptism.* Philadelphia: Wm. Rutter, 1871.

————. *Christic and Patristic Baptism.* Philadelphia: Presby. Brd. of Pubn., 1874.

————. *Classic Baptism.* Philadelphia: Presby. Brd. of Pubn., 1867.

Dana, H. E., and Mantey, J. R. *A Manual Grammar of the Greek New Testament.* New York: Macmillan, 1939.

Dibelius, Otto. *Die Werdende Kirsche: Eine Einführing in die Apostelgeschichte.* Hamburg: Im Furche Verlag, 1951.

Dixon, A. C. *The Person and Ministry of the Holy Spirit.* London: Dickinson, 1891.

Dolman, H. D. *Simple Talks on the Holy Spirit.* New York: Revell, 1927.

Downer, Arthur T. *The Mission and Ministration of the Holy Spirit.* Edinburgh: T. & T. Clark, 1909.

Downie, H. K. *Harvest Festivals.* New York: Loizeaux, 1951.

Duffield, Guy Jr. *Pentecostal Preaching.* New York: Vantage, 1957.

Dunn, James. *The Baptism in the Holy Spirit: A Reexamination of the New Testament Teaching on the Gift of the Spirit in Relation to Pentecostalism Today.* Naperville, Ill.: Alec Alenson, 1970.

Ellis, F. M. *The Person and Ministry of the Holy Spirit.* Ed. A. C. Dixon. London: Dickinson, 1891.

English, E. Schuyler. *Studies in the Epistle to the Colossians.* New York: "Our Hope," 1944.

Entzminger, Louis. *The Baptism with the Holy Spirit and Tongues.* Houston, Tex: Louis Entzminger, 1938.

Epp, Theodore. "The Bible or Experience?" *Christian Victory Magazine* 47 (April 1973): 14.

Erdman, Charles R. *The Spirit of Christ.* New York: Doran, 1926.

Erwin, Howard M. *These Are Not Drunken, As Ye Suppose.* Plainfield, N.J.: Logos Internat., 1968.

Ewing, W. "Samaritans." In *International Standard Bible Encyclopaedia,* ed. James Orr. Grand Rapids: Eerdmans, 1939.

Faber, G. S. *A Practical Treatise on the Ordinary Operations of the Holy Spirit.* London: Rivington, 1834.

Fairfield, Edmund B. *Letters on Baptism.* Richmond, Va.: Methodist-Episcopal Pub., 1925.

Figart, Thomas O. "The Filling of the Spirit." *Christian Victory Magazine* 47 (April 1973).

Finlayson, R. A. *"Baptism of the Holy Spirit."* In *Encyclopedia of Christianity,* ed. E. H. Palmer. Wilmington, Del.: Nat. Found. for Chr. Ed., 1964.

Finney, Charles G. *Memoirs.* New York: Revell, 1903.

Frost, Henry W. *Who Is the Holy Spirit?* New York: Revell, 1938.

Gaebelein, A. C. *The Annotated Bible.* 9 vols. New York: "Our Hope," 1916.

———. *The Gospel of Matthew.* New York: "Our Hope," 1910.

———. *The Acts of The Apostles.* New York: "Our Hope," n.d.

Gee, Donald. *The Pentecostal Movement.* London: Elim, 1949.

————. *Pentecost: A Quarterly Review of Worldwide Pentecostal Activity,* no. 45 (September 1958).

————. *God's Great Gift.* Springfield, Mo.: Gospel Pub., n.d.

————. *Concerning Spiritual Gifts: A Series of Bible Studies.* Springfield, Mo.: Gospel Pub., 1947.

Goodman, Montague. *The Comforter.* London: Paternoster, 1938.

Goodwin, John. *A Being Filled with the Holy Spirit.* Edinburgh: James Nichol, 1967.

Gordon, A. J. *The Ministry of the Spirit.* New York: Revell, 1894.

Gordon, S. D. *Quiet Talks on Power.* New York: Revell, 1903.

Grant, F. W. *The Numerical Bible.* New York: Loizeaux, 1913.

Green, James B. *Studies in the Holy Spirit.* New York: Revell, 1936.

Gromacki, Robert G. *The Modern Tongues Movement.* Nutley, N.J.: Presby. & Ref., 1967.

Grounds, Vernon C. "Understanding the Neo-Mystical Movement." *Christian Heritage Magazine,* January 1973, pp. 4-7.

Haldeman, I. M. *The Truth About Baptism.* New York: Haldeman, n.d.

————. *Holy Ghost Baptism and Speaking with Tongues.* New York: Haldeman, n.d.

————. *Holy Ghost or Water?* New York: Haldeman, n.d.

Hare, J. C. *The Mission of the Comforter.* London: Macmillan, 1877.

Harper, Michael. *As at the Beginning: The Twentieth-Century Pentecostal Revival.* London: Hodder & Stoughton, 1965.

Harrison, Norman B. *His Very Own: Paul's Epistle to the Ephesians.* Chicago: BICA, 1930.

Hawes, E. E. *Baptism Mode Studies.* Richmond, Va.: Whittet & Shepherson, 1857.

Hendrix, Eugene R. *The Personality of the Holy Spirit.* Nashville: Methodist-Episcopal Pub., 1905.

Hicks, R. C. *The Baptism of Jesus.* Nashville: Smith & Lamarr, 1909.

Hodges, Melvin L. *Spiritual Gifts.* Springfield, Mo.: Gospel Pub., 1964.

Hodges, Zane C. "The Purpose of Tongues." *Bibliotheca Sacra,* July-September 1963, pp. 226-33.

Hoekema, Anthony. *Holy Spirit Baptism.* Grand Rapids: Eerdmans, 1972.

Horton, Harold. *The Gifts of the Spirit.* Rev. ed. Bedfordshire, England: Redemption Tidings, 1946.

Huegel, F. J. *Bone of His Bone.* Grand Rapids: Zondervan, n.d.

Hughes, Ray H. *What Is Pentecost?* Cleveland, Tenn.: Pathway, 1968.

Humphries, A. Lewis. *The Holy Spirit in Faith and Experience.* London: Hammond, 1911.

Ironside, H. A. *Wrongly Dividing The Word of Truth.* New York: Loizeaux, n.d.

————. *The Mission of the Holy Spirit.* New York: Loizeaux, n.d.

Jamieson, R.; Fausset, A. R.; and Brown, R. *A Commentary on the Old and New Testament.* Vol. 2. New York: Scranton, 1893.

Jarvis, E. J. "This Is That." *Pentecostal Evangel* 49 (Jan. 15, 1961): 6-7.

Jenkyn, Thomas W. *The Union of the Holy Spirit and the Church.* Boston: Gould, Kendall, & Lincoln, 1946.

Johnson, E. H. *The Holy Spirit and Now.* Philadelphia: Griffith & Rowland, 1904.

Johnson, S. Lewis. "The Gift of Tongues in the Book of Acts." *Bibliotheca Sacra,* October-December, 1963, pp. 308-31.

Kendrick, Claude. *The Promise Fulfilled: A History of the Modern Pentecostal Movement.* Springfield, Mo.: Gospel Pub., 1961.

Kenyon, John B. *The Bible Revelation of the Holy Spirit.* Grand Rapids: Zondervan, 1939.

Kluepfel, P. *The Holy Spirit in the Life and Teachings of Jesus and the Early Church.* Columbus, Ohio: Lutheran Book Concern, 1929.

Knowling, R. J. "The Acts of the Apostles." In *The Expositor's Greek Testament,* vol. 2, ed. William R. Nicoll. Grand Rapids: Eerdmans, n.d.

Koch, Kurt. *Revival Fires in Canada.* Grand Rapids: Kregel, 1973.

Kuyper, Abraham. *The Work of the Holy Spirit.* Trans. Henri DeVries. New York: Funk & Wagnalls, 1900.

Larkin, Clarence. *Dispensational Truth.* 7th ed. Philadelphia: Clarence Larkin Estate, 1920.

Law, William. *The Power of the Spirit, An Address to the Clergy.* Ed. Andrew Murray. London: James Nisbet, 1896.

Lawson, J. Gilchrist. *Deeper Experiences of Famous Christians.* Springfield, Mo.: Gospel Pub., 1911.

Mahon, Asa. *The Baptism of the Holy Ghost.* New York: Palmer, 1870.

Massee, J. C. *The Holy Spirit.* New York: Revell, 1940.

McConkey, James. *The Three-fold Secret of the Holy Spirit.* Pittsburgh: Silver Pub., 1897.

McCrossan, T. J. *Christ's Paralyzed Church X-Rayed.* Seattle, Wash.: T. J. McCrossan, 1937.

————. *Speaking in Tongues: Sign or Gift—Which?* New York: C&MA, 1927.

McEwen, J. S. *Scottish Journal of Theology* 7 (1954):133-52.

McLoughlin, William G., Jr. *Modern Revivalism: Charles Grandison Finney to Billy Graham.* New York: Ronald, 1959.

Miles, F. J. *The Greatest Unused Power in the World.* Minneapolis: Wilson, 1944.

Morgan, G. Campbell. *The Spirit of God.* New York: Revell, 1900.

————. *The Acts of the Apostles.* New York: Revell, 1924.

————. *The Corinthian Letters of Paul.* New York: Revell, 1924.

Morris, Leon. *The Gospel According to John.* The New International Commentary on the New Testament, ed. F. F. Bruce. Grand Rapids: Eerdmans, 1971.

Moule, Handley C. G. *Ephesian Studies.* London: Thynne, n.d.

————. *Veni, Creator: Thoughts on the Person and Work of the Holy Spirit of Promise.* London: Hodder & Stoughton, 1890.

Neill, S. C. *Toward Church Union, 1937-1952.* Chicago: Allenson, 1952.

————. "Ecumenical Movement." In *Encyclopedia Britannica.*

Nichols, J. T. *Pentecostalism.* New York: Harper & Row, 1966.

O'Rear, Arthur T. *The Nativity of the Holy Spirit.* Louisville, Ky.: Pentecostal Pub., 1929.

Owen, John. *A Discourse Concerning the Holy Spirit.* Vols. 1 & 2. Glasgow: A. Macauley, P. Mair, 1791.

Pache, René. *The Person and Work of the Holy Spirit.* Chicago: Moody, 1954.

Pardington, George P. *The Crisis of the Deeper Life.* New York: C&MA, 1925.

Parker, Joseph. *The Paraclete: The Holy Ghost.* London: Henry S. King, 1874.

Plumptre, E. H. *A New Testament Commentary for English Readers*. Ed. C. J. Ellicott. New York: Cassell, Petter, Galpin, 1883.

Ranaghan, Kevin and Dorothy. *Catholic Pentecostals*. Paramus, N.J.: Paulist Press, Deus Books, 1969.

Rees, T. *The Holy Spirit in Thought and Experience*. New York: Scribner, 1915.

Rendall, F. "The Epistle to the Galatians." In *The Expositor's Greek Testament*, vol. 3, ed. William R. Nicoll. Grand Rapids, Eerdmans, n.d.

Rice, John R. *The Power of Pentecost: The Fullness of the Spirit*. Wheaton, Ill.: Sword of the Lord, 1949.

Ridout, S. *The Person and Work of the Holy Spirit*. New York: Loizeaux, n.d.

Riggs, Ralph. *The Spirit Himself*. Springfield, Mo.: Gospel Pub., 1949.

Roads, Charles. *The Full Vision of Pentecost*. Lebanon, Pa.: Sowers Printing, 1937.

Robertson, A. T. *A Grammar of the Greek New Testament in the Light of Historical Research*. 4th ed. New York: Hodder & Stoughton, 1928.

Rouse, R., and Neill, S. C., eds. *A History of the Ecumenical Movement 1517-1948*. London: SPCK, 1954.

Salmond, S. D. F. "The Epistle to the Ephesians." In *The Expositor's Greek Testament*, vol. 3, ed. William R. Nicoll. Grand Rapids: Eerdmans, n.d.

Schaeffer, Francis. "Beware of the New Super-Spirituality." *Eternity*, November 1972.

Schmidt, Kurt D. "Luthers Lehre vom Heiligen Geist." *Schrift und Bekenntnis: Zeugnisse Lutheranische Theologie*. Hamburg: im Furchte Verlag, 1950.

Scofield, C. I. *Rightly Dividing the Word of Truth*. New York: Revell, n.d.

————, ed. *New Scofield Reference Bible*. New York: Oxford, 1967.

Sherrill, John. *They Speak with Other Tongues*. Westwood, N.J.: Revell, 1964.

Simpson, A. B. *The Holy Spirit, or Power from on High*. New York: Christian Alliance, 1895.

Simpson, E. K. *Commentary on the Epistle to the Ephesians*. New International Bible Commentary on the New Testament. Grand Rapids: Eerdmans, 1972.

Smeaton, George. *The Doctrine of the Holy Spirit*. Edinburgh: T. & T. Clark, 1882.

Smith, A. A. *The Holy Spirit and His Workings*. Tampa, Florida: A. A. Smith, 1934.

Soltau, George. *The Person and Mission of the Holy Spirit*. Philadelphia: Phila. Sch. of Bible, n.d.

Stam, Cornelius. *The Fundamentals of Dispensationalism*. Milwaukee: Berean Searchlight, 1951.

Stedman, Ray C. "One Baptism." *Our Hope Magazine* 59 (1952).

Stott, John R. *The Baptism and Fullness of the Spirit*. Downers Grove, Ill.: Inter-Varsity, 1971.

Strombeck, J. F. *First the Rapture*. Moline, Ill.: Strombeck, 1950.

Swete, Henry Barclay. *The Holy Spirit in the Ancient Church: A Study of Christian Teaching in the Age of the Fathers*. New York: Macmillan, 1912.

―――. *Early History of the Doctrine of the Holy Spirit*. Cambridge: Deighton, 1873.

―――. *The Holy Spirit in the New Testament*. New York: Macmillan, 1909.

Tenney, Merrill C. *John: The Gospel of Belief*. Grand Rapids: Eerdmans, 1948.

Thayer, J. H. *Greek-English Lexicon of the New Testament*. New York: American Book, 1889.

Thomas, W. H. Griffith. *The Holy Spirit of God*. Chicago: BICA, 1913.

―――. *Grace and Power*. Grand Rapids: Eerdmans, 1949.

Torrey, R. A. *What the Bible Teaches*. London: James Nisbet, 1898.

―――. *The Baptism with the Holy Spirit*. New York: Revell, 1895.

Unger, Merrill F. *The New Testament Teaching on Tongues*. Grand Rapids: Kregel, 1971.

―――. *Unger's Bible Handbook*. Chicago: Moody, 1972.

―――. *The Baptizing Work of the Holy Spirit*. Findlay, Ohio: Dunham, 1962.

―――. *Demons in the World Today*. Wheaton, Ill.: Tyndale, 1970.

Van Gorder, Paul. *Cure for Charismatic Confusion*. Grand Rapids: Radio Bible Class, 1972.

Vaughn, C. R. *The Gifts of the Holy Spirit to Unbelievers and Believers*. Richmond, Va.: Presby. Com. of Pub., 1874.

Visser 'T Hooft, W. A. *The Meaning of Ecumenical.* Petersborough, N.H.: Bauhan, William, 1954.

Walvoord, John F. *The Doctrine of the Holy Spirit.* Dallas: Dallas Sem., 1943.

Warfield, B. B. *Counterfeit Miracles.* New York: Scriveners, 1918.

Webb, Allen B. *The Presence and Office of the Holy Spirit.* 8th ed. London: Skeffington & Son, 1889.

Wesley, John. *A Plain Account of Christian Perfection.* London: Epworth, 1952.

Westcott, Brooke Foss. *St. Paul's Epistle to the Ephesians.* New York: Macmillan, 1906.

Williams, Ernest S. *Systematic Theology.* 3 vols. Springfield, Mo.: Gospel Pub., 1953.

―――. "Your Questions," *Pentecostal Evangel* 49 (1961).

Winehouse, Irwin. *The Assemblies of God: A Popular Survey.* New York: Vantage, 1959.

Wolston, W. T. P. *Another Comforter.* 2d ed. London: James Nisbet, 1900.

Young, Robert. *Analytical Concordance to the Bible.* 22d Amer. ed. Rev. W. B. Stevens. New York: Funk & Wagnalls, 1936.